The World of
PONIES

The World of
PONIES
Judith Campbell

Hamlyn
London · New York · Sydney · Toronto

Published by
THE HAMLYN PUBLISHING GROUP LIMITED
London · New York · Sydney · Toronto
Hamlyn House, Feltham, Middlesex, England
© Copyright The Hamlyn Publishing Group 1970
Reprinted 1971

ISBN   0 600 03978 1

Printed in Italy by Arnoldo Mondadori Editore, Verona

Contents

Pony breeds

The native ponies of Iceland are intelligent, tough and comfortable to ride

Horses and ponies are of course descended from the same root-stock, originating from four-toed, fox-sized little creatures that lived in prehistoric times. Today's many different breeds and types were evolved through the centuries, partly through the influence of terrain and climate, and more recently through the needs of mankind.

For many years the standard definition of a pony was 'a horse of any small breed not more than 13 hands high or popularly 14 hands high', but the difference between horses and ponies is certainly not purely one of size. To begin with the height limit varies quite widely. In modern British showing classes a Hackney pony must not exceed 14 hands, British show ponies and show jumping ponies have a maximum height limit of 14 hands 2 inches (with a half inch allowance for shoes) and since 1966 the National Pony Society has accepted registration of ponies for breeding purposes up to 15·2 hands. All over the world the beautiful Arabian is classified as a horse, yet it can be well below 14 hands.

A true pony is characterized by a compact body, neat head with small, sharp-pricked ears, and a definite pony expression, difficult to define but quite unlike that of a horse. Ponies are tougher creatures than most breeds of horses being closer to their common wild ancestors, and through an ancient heritage of fending for themselves on moorland and mountainside, they have acquired a built-in resistance to disease. They thrive on relatively rough pasture that would be unsuitable for a horse; they are surefooted on the most rugged going and are clever at extricating themselves from awkward situations – which makes a drop of pony blood a sought-after ingredient in an event horse.

Ponies are unlike horses in temperament, being usually more clever, often more mischievous, occasionally more obstinate, and always more adept at getting over, through or under the fences that are supposed to contain them. They are comic, lovable, affectionate, and normally possessed of the qualities as well as size that ensure them becoming part of the family in the shortest possible time.

Each year more families are keeping their own riding animal and for convenience and cost this is most likely to be a pony in Great Britain. A large proportion of these are admirable cross-breds and half-breds and those of untraceable ancestry, but the remainder belong to one of the many different breeds or specific types to be found throughout the modern world.

For geographical reasons small islands often play a part in keeping a particular type of pony free from undesired alien blood. There are few if any breeds today that have not at some time been improved (and occasionally debased) by cross-breeding, but on an island such a policy must be of deliberate intent.

This mare and foal have been rounded up on the island of Assateague and have swum across the Channel for the annual sale

One hundred and eighty miles east of Halifax lies Sable Island, a shrinking nub of windswept beach and dune and shallow lagoon that sits off the coast of Novia Scotia. Forty-five years ago there were about 300 ponies running wild there, fending for themselves just as they do today although the herd is said now to be nearer 200. Their origin is shrouded in mystery, the one common but usually disproved theory being that the ponies are descendants of horses washed ashore from a shipwreck, their stature then blunted by the rigours of their existence. The most likely explanation is that the herd originated from ponies landed by French colonizing expeditions of the sixteenth and seventeenth centuries. They could have been small hardy animals which perhaps developed in a region of the Biscayan coast in the same manner as those of the Camargue. However they evolved, the ponies of Sable Island have altered little in the years they have been under observation by the crew members of the lifesaving station, first established there in 1801. Not so many years ago about a dozen Sable Island ponies used to be captured when needed, trained and stabled and then ridden to patrol the coast during storms and thick weather, or harnessed up to the lifeboat to draw it to the other side of the island. Now fifty or so ponies are caught annually and shipped to the mainland for sale, to ensure that the herd does not outgrow its meagre grazing.

For the same reason another sale of island ponies takes place on the last Thursday and Friday of each July. On the previous day the

*Connemaras are good natured and
jump well. They make splendid
mounts for children and adults*

*This Exmoor foal, like most native
ponies living semi-wild, is branded
with its owner's mark*

channel dividing the islands of Assateague and Chincoteague off
the Virginian coast of America, is dotted with the heads of swimming ponies. They are mostly piebald and skewbald little animals
which have lived on the islands since early colonial times. It has
now become traditional to round up a number of them on un-
inhabited Assateague and swim them across to join up with those
collected on Chincoteague, for an annual auction sale.

Up to sixty years ago there were more than 1,000 little ponies of
an ancient breed roaming the Greek island of Skyros. However,
poor pasture, lack of minerals and parasitic disease reduced their
natural hardiness and threatened to exterminate them. In 1969 the
Greek Ministry of Agriculture together with local island authori-
ties and a registered British Charity, the Greek Animal Welfare
Fund, joined forces to save the remnant of the herd. About 100
have survived, including twenty-five or so which are used for light
work by the islanders. All but these graze in the mountains, and
now land has been allocated for a winter corral and the Ministry is
piping water to the area, fencing it and providing shelter. Capital
for the initial scheme produced by voluntary contributions to the
Welfare Fund, is also stretched to include winter fodder for some
years. Only the pure-bred feral ponies are included in the plan and
their breeding is now being supervised. In time the scheme should
become self-supporting as the Skyros ponies help to attract more
tourists to the island.

A spectacular round-up of Iceland ponies

Iceland ponies are descended from those brought by settlers from Norway and the Western Isles in the ninth century. Attempts have been made to produce a lighter pony for children by introducing Thoroughbred blood, but these have been unsuccessful. Iceland ponies remain true to type, retaining the exceptional hardiness that enables them to thrive under the most rigorous natural conditions. They are noted for their good temper and distinct comfortable gait which endear them to the increasing number of summer visitors who explore the wild attractions of Iceland with their aid. After a trek the ponies are sometimes loosed but their strong homing instinct always guarantees their safe return to base within twenty-four hours.

One British trekking centre at Penrith has discovered that it pays to import some of its ponies from Iceland. They find Iceland ponies sturdy animals and added inducements are their surefootedness and reliability, the ponies remaining literally unmoved even if a rider falls off. Their docile nature makes it possible to take even child beginners on exciting treks through the craggy beauty of the Lakeland hills.

Skoggesbagge (meaning a small ram living in the woods) and Russ are both old names for the Gotland pony of Sweden. Long

Shetland ponies thrive in the harsh surroundings of their native isles

A Highland stallion in show tack

15

Haflinger ponies are native to Austria. They are a typical mountain breed, strong, short in the leg and very sure-footed

ago hundreds of these ponies did indeed run wild and breed in the woods, often far from sight or sound of man. The best were rounded up each year, some for children's mounts, some to give milk on the farms, and from the nineteenth century about 200 were annually exported to England, Belgium and Germany for work in the mines. Because of decreasing numbers steps were taken to conserve the breed, and quality and uniformity improved. Today Russ ponies are bred by numbers of farmers, and a small herd is kept on the island of Gotland where they still run more or less wild but are in the care of the Swedish Board of Agriculture.

When Lundy, a small island off the Devon coast, came up for sale in 1969, there were rumours of pop groups or casino chiefs taking it over. However, through the generosity of an Englishman living in the USA, the National Trust acquired the island with its short-cropped turf jewelled with wild flowers among the bramble-covered outcrops of granite, ensuring for all time the safety of the wild birds, the seals, the Soay sheep, the feral goats and the herd of about twenty ponies that live there.

Lundy ponies began with thirty-four supposedly in foal New Forest mares with eight foals at foot, imported and turned loose in 1928. In fact no foals were born, a subsequently imported Thoroughbred stallion proved infertile, and by the time an ex-champion Welsh entire remedied the situation, only twenty-seven mares remained. Herd numbers were stabilized by drafting the culls and colt suckers each autumn, but no livestock could be shipped off the island during the last war, and over-crowding, grazing shortage, and fighting among the young pony stallions became acute.

Since those days various island-bred stallions have been retained for breeding and outside blood has also been introduced. This has included a Welsh cob, the Connemara that is now resident stallion, and a half-bred hunter called Surprise – which lived up to its name by refusing to have anything to do with any mare that was grey, palomino or albino. These Lundy ponies cannot be called a breed, but are a type of good repute for their amiable temperaments, inbuilt jumping ability, hardiness, and exceptionally good hooves kept in excellent shape by the sharp quartz in the granite outcrops of their island home.

Pedar, the present Lundy stallion, is himself of island stock since Connemaras are truly indigenous to Ireland. Their origin is un-known but the shipwreck legend crops up once more, suggesting that Connemara ponies owe some of their quality to stallions that swam ashore from wrecks of the Spanish armada. It is more likely that the ponies carry the blood of those ambling, highly prized Spanish Jennets – the result of crossing indigenous Spanish horses with the Barbs and Arabians brought to Spain during the Saracen

There are plenty of ponies running wild on Dartmoor although nowadays many of them are not pure-bred

Shetland brood mare in Germany

Below
Exmoor ponies

Bottom
The virtues of Connemaras have been known in Ireland, their land of origin, for many centuries. Now these excellent ponies are becoming universally popular.

Fell ponies are docile with children and plenty strong enough to carry an adult

invasions. These found their way to Ireland when Galway was trading regularly with Spain during the Middle Ages. Arabian blood has occasionally been reintroduced up to the present day.

As far back as the end of the nineteenth century a royal commission was noting the wiry ponies in the west of Galway with their good legs and action, great stamina, intelligence, easy paces, and capacity for work. However, Connemaras have only quite recently become well known outside their country of origin, and recognized as wonderful ponies for riding and jumping by both children and light-weight adults. They are now bred extensively in England and are finding favour in many countries including Germany, Scandinavia, the USA, Hawaii, New Zealand, and Australia where the progeny of Island King, the first imported Connemara stallion, are now helping to popularize the breed. Two of the most famous Irish Connemara studs are situated on small islands – on Lambay four miles off the Irish coast, and fifty miles west near Lough Mask on a lake island, from which the ponies are swum back to the mainland as required in the wake of a row-boat.

Connemaras are one of the larger breeds of pony, but Shetlands are the smallest breed bar one. This exception is the Felabella, at most only 30 inches high at maturity and usually between 24 and 28 inches. The Felabella has been bred for some years on a ranch outside Buenos Aires where the herd, now numbering about 400, runs on the pampas. Senor Felabella evolved these tiny ponies by breeding down, using the smallest crosses of Shetland with Argentine ponies, and they now breed true.

Felabellas were introduced into England about twelve years ago and attracted a lot of interest. Too small for riding by children over six years old, these little creatures make good pets and are used for drawing miniature driving turn-outs, their gentle nature and elegant good-looks making them particularly popular in North America. One British family often grazes its Felabella foals and yearlings on the lawn and is no longer surprised to discover that the ponies have found their way indoors, and are curled up on the sitting-room chairs and sofa.

Shetlands, the rootstock of these ponies, are one of the most ancient, picturesque and strongest breeds for their size in the world. They originate from the Shetland group of islands north-east of the Scottish mainland, their known record going back some 2,000 years. The Shetland's small size and thick, shaggy coat fits it for the sparse grazing and harsh climate of its native home. In the islands the ponies include seaweed in their diet when necessary. Even when living on lush grazing far from their natural habitat, Shetlands seldom grow above 40 inches.

These ponies are popular in Holland where they have been bred for some years, and Shetland pony breeding is booming in Germany. Belgium, Denmark and Australia include Shetlands among their pony studs, and they are one of the breeds recognized by the Canadian Pony Society. There are three types of Shetland bred in the USA, for riding, draught and harness events, including roadster and fine harness classes in which the animals wear false hooves. Their active action and size in show classes indicates the introduction of Hackney blood during their breeding.

The other Scottish breed of pony, the Highland, was known until recently principally for the esteem in which Queen Victoria held it, and for its strength and reliability in carrying carcasses of stags across the deer forests of Scotland. Hundreds of these ponies, often erroneously called 'Garrons' (from the Gaelic meaning a cut horse or gelding) are used north of the border for trekking, but their good qualities and all-round uses are taking them nowadays to many countries in the world. They are rugged enough to be used on Exmoor for rounding up sheep but crosses with Thoroughbred,

Shetland ponies are probably the oldest and hardiest of Britain's native breeds

*Fjord ponies from Norway are used
for many kinds of work all over
Scandinavia*

Felabellas originated in the Argentine and are the smallest ponies in the world

All ponies need plenty of water to drink, and there is certainly no lack of it in the New Forest.

New Forest ponies having their tails shortened to show that tail fees have been paid for the grazing rights

There are bargains for the know-ledgeable at the annual New Forest pony sales

Anglo-Arab or Arabian stock will produce animals with good bone and temperament. It is also interesting to note that the famous event horse High and Mighty had a Highland grandmother.

Highlands come in two types, the Western Island pony being smaller and lighter than the mainland pony, although they are now much interbred and both are capable of holding their own at work ranging from dragging wood to driving or hunting.

Dales and Fell, the other two large breeds of British pony, were originally distinct only by district, the Dales coming from the upper dales of Allen, Tyne, Wear and Tees, and the Fell from Westmorland and Cumberland. They are both strong, weight-carrying types with a history of hard work hauling loads of lead to and from the northern mines. An infusion of Clydesdale blood has made the Dales a larger, heavier pony than the Fell and turned it into a true utility pony for the dales farmer – equally at home ploughing, carting, or carrying its owner shepherding on the hills. Fell ponies are usually about a hand smaller than the Dales, averaging about 13·2 hands. Their heritage as pack ponies has given them an especially good, sure-footed walk and their friendly disposition makes them suitable for children to ride.

The Fell ponies on the royal estate at Balmoral now have two aliens working with them as deer ponies, Franzi and Trista, the pair of Haflinger mares presented to Queen Elizabeth II during her state visit to Austria in 1969. Not very tall but extremely strong, these attractive cream ponies with the dark eel stripe running down their backs, are named after a village near Meran in the South Tyrol. Haflingers go back to 1837 and are descended from small indigenous ponies crossed with the Arabian stallion El Bedavi. They are also found in Germany and Bavaria and in Italy where they are known as Avelignese.

There have been ponies running more or less wild in the British Isles since time immemorial and New Forest ponies are mentioned in the Domesday Book. Culled naturally by sparse grazing and wet, bleak winters the ponies of the forest have always been exceptionally hardy, but through the introduction at various times of different breeds of stallion, they are less typed than other British ponies. A policy of selective breeding using stallions within the breed has produced ponies with stamina, good temperaments, cow hocks, low set tails, long ears, large heads and a most useful moustache to protect the lips when feeding on prickly gorse. Today's New Forest ponies come in two sizes – those up to 13·2 hands which are lighter in bone but most suitable as children's quality hunters, and the larger animals up to 14·2 hands which are capable of carrying light adults with ease. Both types have been bred away from the less attractive aspects of the old forest pony, but retain their versatility, hardiness, pleasant natures and an inbuilt indifference to traffic

Round-up in the New Forest prior to the pony sales

With light-coloured muzzles and underparts and the same mealy colouring round the eyes, Exmoor ponies are unmistakable

produced by years of familiarity with cars. Casualties among the forest ponies have become so heavy that in the interests of both animals and humans, most of the forest roads are now fenced.

In 1909 the New Forest stallion Burton Sligo was sent to Australia, but the export of these ponies really began in 1955 when the three-year-old filly champion at Lymington Show was sent to the USA. In 1961 a four-year-old was bought for the children of the King of Nepal. Three hundred and twenty-two New Forest ponies were exported to Denmark two years later, and the Royal Danish Master of Horse now has a thriving stud of the larger type. These ponies are popular in Sweden, and there is a steady export trade to Germany and France. The market, however, continues to grow more difficult as Continental breeders produce their own stock.

Fortunately when Henry VIII, influenced by his own girth and the needs of his cavalry, ordered the slaughter of all horse sires less than 14 hands, many native ponies escaped the edict – saved by the

Exmoor ponies at Bampton Fair

remote regions in which they lived and by the serfs and peasants who were unable to feed larger animals.

For centuries the high bleak moorlands of Exmoor have provided a natural refuge for herds of small ponies with distinctive mealy coloured muzzles and wiry winter coats, that have run wild and bred true longer than any other British breed. In Canada they are making a great name for themselves, and one Canadian breeder has sold his entire herd of Exmoors to the USA.

Another type of small pony was inhabiting the savage tors and dangerous bogs of nearby Dartmoor way back in 1012. Used between the twelfth and fifteenth centuries for carrying tin off the moors, and later for farm work, Dartmoor ponies have since run free – sustaining themselves entirely and scratching beneath the snow for food in winter. With the demand in the nineteenth and early twentieth centuries for small pit ponies, Shetland stallions were introduced on the moor, a cross that still persists. However,

Dartmoors are bred pure on many studs, and are recognized both in England and overseas as the best possible riding pony for young children and as foundation stock for breeding larger ponies.

Three hundred miles north and 4,500 feet up from the steaming heat of Panama City, a herd of Welsh Mountain ponies roams and thrives in a region as rocky and arduous as their true home land. These handsome little ponies with their distinctive 'look of eagles' derived originally from an infusion of Arabian blood, command high prices and acclaim in many countries in the world. In height up to 12 hands, the modern Welsh Mountain is smaller than its predecessors and the riding type lacks some of the high-stepping action evolved, according to legend, for picking their way along the rough mountain tracks of Wales and over stones in the darkness of a coal mine. Acknowledged as the world's most beautiful pony, this mountain breed is sought after as children's first ponies, and for the harness work in driving classes that are so popular in the USA and Canada, and rapidly growing in popularity in Britain.

The Welsh Mountain is the foundation stock of the larger Welsh pony – a true riding type, the less well-known small Cob type and the Welsh Cob – a compact, fiery-looking weight carrier that combines prowess in the hunting field with the qualities of a first-class driving animal.

The Welsh Mountain is the rootstock of section B and C Welsh ponies and of the Welsh Cob

The Fjords, Norway's native ponies, are also excellent in harness, and can be seen scurrying along at their own particular tireless, shuffling trot, drawing low carts with four wheels or the smaller cajol, where two passengers sit one behind the other. In looks, Fjord ponies are very unlike Welsh ponies. They have small truncated ears, short, very strong necks, and cream or dun colouring with a dark dorsal stripe running from tail to forelock right through the upright, clipped mane. Friendly, hardworking and docile, these ponies are never blanketed against the biting cold and thrive on hay alone, even when working on heavy timber haulage. In winter they usually share a communal stable with pigs, cattle and other livestock.

Many of the Dülmen ponies – the so-called wild horses first mentioned in a document of 1316 – that now run free on a preserve on the edge of the Ruhr in Germany, carry the same dorsal stripe. The fame of the annual round-up of these ponies brings visitors of many nationalities flocking to the old town of Dülmen – some purely as spectators, and some to bid for the young stock which on maturity go well in harness and make good ponies for children.

There are feral horses and ponies in the Lake Taupo district of New Zealand, descendants of a few stallions that escaped in the nineteenth century to join some wild mares. Grazing tussock and monoau scrub, flax and swamp grass, these ponies now possess great stamina and are valued as stock ponies by the Maoris who

The spotted Appaloosas are a recognized breed in the USA

officially own them. Today the herds have been diminished by capture and encroaching civilization, and the remnants are hard to find among the afforestation projects undertaken by successive governments.

Some of the geuine New Zealand ponies come from Australia and are either of the increasingly popular British breeds, or one of Australia's native types. These Australian ponies, descended from riding ponies imported from Britain have their own stud book and separate classes at many Australian shows. Most ponies between 14 and 15 hands are a type called Galloway, which have a variety of their own show classes.

In the western states particularly, there are strains of Timor pony, mostly mousy-brown or dun with black eel stripes. Not perhaps very high class, these thick-set little ponies are very active and make admirable all-rounders for children. Many Australian show ponies display Arabian characteristics, but are seldom like the miniature Thoroughbreds frequently seen in Britain. They are true ponies with a quality that is improving yearly, frequently more sensible and suitable than the beautiful but too often hot blood ponies.

Horses cannot be kept in parts of Africa because of tsetse fly, but there are at least three types of pony in Ethiopia. The Eritrean, bred in the semi-deserts of the west and close to the Sudan, usually has an obvious intake of Arabian blood. The Ethiopian or Abyssinian pony of the central plateau is a mountain animal, unappreciative of the lowland heat unlike the similar Boran, which can travel long distances day after day in the soaring temperatures of the southern plains.

Fifty or so years ago almost the only ponies found in Kenya were the sturdy little Borans, bought by the settlers from tribesmen who trekked the ponies down from southern Ethiopia. The Kenyans soon discovered that Boran mares crossed with Thoroughbred sires produced excellent progeny, and many of Kenya's racehorses are descended from this almost humble beginning.

The Basuto is the best known African pony although, through many years of inertia and breeding from inferior sires, the modern Basuto is far removed from those animals that became widely famed during the Boer War. Although they lack the quality of their predecessors, Basuto ponies still thrive on minimum fare, and retain the ability to gallop faster and with more courage up and down precipitous slopes than any other breed.

Basuto ponies are descended from the renowned Cape horse, a breed of predominantly oriental blood that originated from four animals from Java, landed in the Cape by the Dutch East India Company in 1653. Border raids and Zulu invasions introduced the ponies into Lesotho, then called Basutoland, until by 1870 practi-

This little Caspian pony stallion has just been racing, but quietens at once to the requirements of his young rider

An Australian trio that are part Welsh Mountain part Arab. Many British native breeds of pony are exported to other countries.

Timor ponies were imported into Australia in the nineteenth century. They may not be beautiful but make tough all-rounders for children.

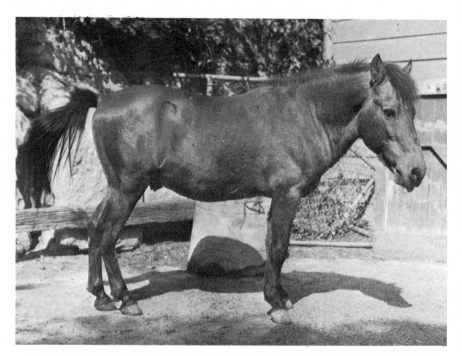

cally the entire Basuto nation was mounted. The ponies became a definite type, their inherited oriental characteristics, small size, endurance and fearlessness accentuated by the mountainous country and the fast, intrepid riding of their Basuto owners.

Persian horses figured largely in the ancestors of the Cape horse, but there is little or no resemblance between Basuto ponies and the small type of pony discovered in Iran during the 1960s. These were called Caspian ponies by the American born Mrs Firouz, who discovered some of the remaining few in their natural habitat, the Amol-Shahi area south of the Caspian Sea, where they were known locally as Mouleki or Pouseki.

With no selective breeding taking place, and being considered of little importance in Iran, this breed of poor man's donkey, used chiefly for hauling large loads through the twisting alleys of local bazaars, had little chance of survival. However, Mrs Firouz, excited by the definite characteristics of long legs and neck, small ears, prominent eyes and fine bone structure, started up a small stud on a farm near Tehran. She found that these little ponies, which range from 10·1 to 11·3 hands high, have exceptionally gentle natures for all their spirited looks, and make excellent riding ponies for young children. Even the stallions are reliable and kind, and will take part in a children's race on the track at Tehran racecourse, and then quieten immediately the excitement of the gallop is over.

Jehan, one of Mrs Firouz's Caspian pony stallions is now standing in America, so that the United States can claim to have

Scots Greys Captain, a versatile Canadian Pony-of-the-Americas, is equally at home show jumping, pony trotting or drawing a sleigh

the two extremes – a representative of possibly one of the most ancient breeds of pony in the world, and ponies of what is certainly the youngest breed – the Pony-of-the-Americas, known as P.O.A.s, evolved only in the past fifteen years or so.

According to a quote in the 1962 issue of the Milwaukee Sentinel, a P.O.A. should have 'The surefooted agility of a goat, stamina of a mule, disposition of a puppy and intelligence of a cow pony'. The breed was evolved originally because the children of the Mason City attorney who later began the Pony-of-the-Americas Club liked the spotted and blanket colouring of their father's Appaloosa horses, and were having trouble with their own Shetland ponies. An Appaloosa mare was crossed with a Shetland stallion, and since then P.O.A.s are usually obtained by the same cross, or by using Welsh or similar quality ponies instead of Shetland.

The result is a small, sturdy animal that ranges between 11·5 and 13 hands, strong enough to carry sixteen-year-olds, handy, intelligent and equable, and resembling a miniature Quarter horse with some Arabian characteristics and the eye-catching colouring of an Appaloosa.

These ponies are remarkably versatile, and distinguish themselves at anything from trail riding to show jumping. They are becoming popular in many countries, particularly in Mexico and in Canada – where the celebrated P.O.A. Scots Greys Captain, bred from an inexpensive Appaloosa mare by John Cusack of the 'Three C' Ranch, achieved a five foot leap during his outstandingly successful show jumping career.

Working ponies

The pony stood motionless while a young boy, his legs dangling and useless, was lifted from its back and returned to the wheelchair that until the previous week had been his only means of loco-motion. Another pony waited patiently while an attractive teen-ager with the mind of an eight-year-old and the unco-ordinated movements of the severely spastic, was encouraged in the difficult feat of dismounting. A third rider, whose thought, speech and limbs had been slowed by a car accident, smiled triumphantly as she slid down unaided, and led her cob off to its box. These are just three of the numbers of disabled children in the world to whom ponies are opening up new horizons.

Inspired by Madame Liz Hartnell who, despite crippling polio paralysis became a famous Olympic dressage rider, 'Riding for the Disabled' originated in Scandinavia some years ago. Even if available, the sport is not suitable for every handicapped person, but doctors and physiotherapists are now convinced of its benefits for many of their patients. Where physical improvement is mini-mal, there is always the sheer joy and sense of achievement in moving around on a pony.

There are centres in Canada and Australia, and recently the representative of an American foundation devoted to the scheme was in England gathering more ideas. In New Zealand members of the Central Hawkes Bay Pony Club lend their most reliable ponies on alternate Sundays, so that the children at the Pukeora Home for the Handicapped may enjoy the pleasure of riding instruction. In Kenya the Kabete Pony Club run a weekly class for disabled children. Each Christmas members ride out together singing carols, to collect funds for the various establishments run by the Association for the Physically Handicapped.

An advisory council was set up in England in 1964 and now there are many affiliated groups throughout the country, the majority run through the generosity and co-operation of riding schools. The Queen has given permission for a group to meet once a week in term-time, at the covered school in the Royal Mews at Buckingham Palace. Another uses the facilities of the Equestrian Centre at Stoneleigh, where Princess Anne, on an official visit in 1969, was delighted to see the children with their dedicated helpers and comic miscellany of ponies. She watched the instruction, and then enjoyed the fun and excitement of a game of mounted 'grand-mother's steps'. Now in many regions there are ponies taking disabled children to explore the wonders of green fields and woodland, sometimes for the first time in their lives.

Medical consent is essential for each rider, and physiotherapists attend many of the sessions. Almost all instruction is given volun-tarily – in Surrey some mounted policemen teach in their spare time – and it is vastly rewarding, but being a qualified riding

Ponies do a wonderful job taking disabled riders out into the open air

instructor is not enough. The job calls for limitless patience and imagination, combined with firmness, the ability to adjust to a slow tempo, and a real appreciation of the capabilities and limitations of each child and pony.

The ponies must be reliable, sure-footed, and willing to stand still. Two helpers, one to lead, one walking beside the rider (three are needed for particularly handicapped children), are mostly drawn from rotas of child- and pony-loving women, happy to give their spare time. The ponies are equipped with neck-straps, leading reins, and check reins, essential for preventing disconcerting head lunging. Saddles have hand grips in front of the bow, and drooping feet are kept in position with clog stirrups. Each child wears a belt with loops, invaluable for grabbing in an emergency, and portable mounting blocks ease the heavy problem of lifting.

In Holland, adult disabled riders learn on Queen Juliana's carriage horses in the Royal Mews at The Hague but, as in other countries, Dutch centres employ ponies for the children. A Norwegian physiotherapist has been giving her young patients riding therapy for years, and imports British native ponies for the job. In Britain at least one group are utilizing sturdy mountain Haflingers, excellent for the heavier children and possessing the equable temperament of ponies that for generations have been part of the Tyrolean farmers' families.

Some ponies are used exclusively for this work, but it is often more satisfactory if they are also ridden by the unhandicapped.

Pantomime ponies rehearse off stage

A number are loaned by members of Pony Clubs but the majority come from riding schools. Dolly, the founder pony of an unusual riding school in Sussex, does this dual job. Unable to keep her Welsh Mountain mare unless she earned her living, Dolly's owner started up what is now called the Pony Kindergarten. Run without other adult help, by, with, and for children, the staff are promoted from the keenest and most efficient pupils. The arrangement works admirably, and there are now ten ponies, ranging from the venerable Dolly to William, a young and sometimes problematical cob originally bred for driving. All the ponies are child- and dog-proof, and sufficiently versatile to act as grooming models for a four-year-old pupil, jump a handy hunter course, or take disabled children quietly around the fields.

Around a quarter of a million people in Great Britain ride every week, and a large proportion of these are catered for by more than 2,000 riding schools licensed under the Riding School Act. This act has done much to curb the type of places where horses and ponies, too often only yearlings or two-year-olds, are kept in tumbledown shacks, under-fed, ill-equipped, badly shod, and hired out to anyone for a nominal sum. However, there are still too few licensed schools, only about 500, that are approved by official

All riding school ponies do admirable work. Pupils from the Sir William Collins school in London are fortunate in that riding is included in the school's curriculum

London coster ponies work hard all the year round, but their good condition is apparent at the annual Easter Parade held by the London Van Horse Parade Society in Regents Park

horse and pony organizations, and there are still too many loopholes; for instance doubtful establishments can avoid licensing altogether by calling themselves livery stables – although there are of course numerous genuine and well run stables of this kind.

Often people who are totally lacking in practical experience set up as riding school proprietors, catering for would-be riders attracted by cut prices and too ignorant to assess either the poor condition of the animals they ride, or the low standard of the so-called instruction. The best safeguard against the existence of such places is to patronize only those schools that are officially approved, and to report any bad ones, whether they are licensed or not.

Good riding schools do a most worth-while job, both for their pupils and for the horses and ponies in their care. At twenty-five years old Dandy is fit and well, and happily engaged in teaching small novices to ride. Once a renowned show jumper, this rotund little pony is far better off employed in a well-run riding school, than turned out to grass deprived of the work and human contact to which he was accustomed, and liable to the foot fever that is the bane of fat, idle, grass-fed ponies.

About 150 miles from Auckland, and inland from where the deep bluey-green Pacific rollers break on the wooded shores of Otarawairere Beach in the Bay of Plenty, is the New Zealand Equestrian Centre. Opened two years ago by a couple of young British horsewomen, it comprises facilities from a jumping paddock and dressage school to a cross-country course with 100 fences, for teaching young and old alike the highest levels of horsemanship. Stable management is also taught, knowledge not always easy to acquire in a land where the majority of horses and ponies are seldom stabled and normally work off grass.

Canadian children have in the past often been confined to riding only within the family property. This was because bridle paths and by-ways were left out in the rapid development of Canadian towns and cities, and because the network of parallel highways that criss-cross the countryside is no place for riders. Added to this, Shetlands were for a long time almost the only ponies in the country and a general belief grew up that all ponies were just pets. The position is very different now, and although there is still some way to go, ponies are rapidly coming into their own. A pioneer school, which teaches that ponies – and children – benefit from proper training, and that ponies can do far more for the young than large horses, was begun in British Columbia in the early 1960s. Mannered riding ponies were impossible to acquire, so the school bought and trained their own young stock, getting by in the meantime with a Shetland or two, and several nice but far too large stock horses.

Riding schools like this were begun way back in 1947 by John Cusack at Mississanga, Ontario, with an original stud of imported Highland and Shetland ponies. Now John Cusack's ranch specializes in most types of pony and light horse, including the famous show jumpers Scots Greys Captain and his progeny, all Ponies-of-the-Americas. Horses, ponies and pupils have the benefit of their instructor's high quality pony and horsemanship which he acquired many years ago at the former admirable British Army Equitation School at Weedon, and further developed serving with the Royal Scots Greys. At his school the accent is on turning youthful riders into practical horsemen, and the success that they and the ponies achieve together is furthering the cause of ponies throughout Canada.

The helpful proprietors of several riding establishments near London, all British Horse Society approved, provide horses and ponies to promote the Inner London Education Authority's excellent decision of 1965, to include riding in their schools' curricula. This involves a growing number of boys and girls, living mostly in the inner parts of the capital, whose former acquaintance with a horse may have been a glimpse of a policeman's mount on street patrol. Many have first to screw up their courage to touch so alien a creature as a pony, let alone ride it. Yet once embarked, these young riders do not waste a second of their precious riding time, and when asked if they intend to continue after leaving school the answer is always yes, whatever else it may mean giving up.

Baby Doll is only a pony, but she is brilliant at roping and other Australian rodeo competitions

Only a few can be included, about 1,000 boys and girls each week from the sixty-six schools included in the scheme, and they usually draw lots for the privilege of learning. The tuition averages one year.

The scheme varies from school to school. At the Sir William Collins School at Kings Cross, where Harry Greenway, French master and enthusiastic horseman, evolved the whole idea, the boys saddle up, ride and, as far as possible look after the same horse or pony on each weekly visit to the riding school. When it comes to the end of term inter-house competitions, fairness is ensured by drawing lots for the available animals.

Much thought goes into the hours of instruction, and into the competitions, to keep all within the bounds of safety to the riders and fairness to the horses and ponies, while providing a real challenge and interest to boys whose more usual enthusiasms lie with football.

That this aim is successful is proved by the good use these pupils make of their limited time and opportunities. It is an inspiration to see the overall keeness; the beautiful, school-designed programmes for the competitions; the noticeably sympathetic hands, and quick, correct reaction to a pony upset by the spectators' thunderous applause. There are creditable performances in Prix Caprilli and double ride competitions, and determined, if not completely successful efforts to get over the fences. When the ponies are ridden bareback for the mounted games, the excitement is heightened by the number of riders who fall off but bounce straight up on to their ponies' backs again as though made of rubber. Each summer a few lucky seniors are taken to benefit from Mr Bryan Young's top-class instruction at Crabbet Park, or to join a Pony Club camp on Exmoor where they can fully realize one of the basic joys of riding – that of partnering a creature of flesh and blood across the untracked ways of the countryside.

Before the advent of hard road surfaces, much of the world's merchandise was carried by pack trains of ponies. Within living memory sturdy ponies driven loose and twenty to a troop, were walked more than 200 miles a week carrying lead across the fells and dales of northern England to the Tyneside docks. They bore their sixteen-stone loads in two panniers slung one on either side, in much the same way that shooting ponies, on some northern and Scottish estates, still bring the day's bag of grouse down off the moors. Despite the ubiquitous Land-Rover, there are still tracts of rough going and treacherous peat hag where sure-footed High-land ponies continue to hold their own, carrying sixteen-stone carcasses of stags, culled during the stalking season from the herds of wild red deer that roam the windswept expanse of the Scottish deer forests.

There are still strings of small, unbelievably tough ponies, almost invisible beneath enormous loads, plodding safely up and down the narrow Himalayan mountain trails, just as they have for centuries. Heads down and short striding, they have the habit, acquired perforce to accommodate the bulky packs, of keeping always to the outside edge of the path. A traveller, venturing among the heights of Kashmir or Nepal on the back of an indis-pensable hill pony, often has the interesting experience of riding with one leg dangling over an abyss.

Mechanization and modern methods have transformed the ancient ways of agriculture, yet even in this age there are still numerous smallholders in many countries, who find willing, economical ponies indispensable to their way of life. In many regions of Scandinavia, Germany, parts of Africa and the Far East, there are ponies working as they have always done. Tucked among the mountains and remote valleys of Wales are farms where ponies and cobs still cart and plough and take the farmer to inspect his hillside sheep. Dalesmen and crofters alike still utilize their native pony breeds; Shetlands, strong despite their size, hump and haul in the islands that bred them, often carrying loads of peat in kelshies – special baskets that hang either side of the wooden saddles or klibbers.

There are still a few Shetlands working in British coal mines. Ten years ago about 11,000 ponies were toiling underground, but the number has been reduced by mechanization at the rate of about

The few remaining pit ponies work under difficult conditions but they receive wonderful care and com-panionship from the miners

The American Pony Express was
short-lived but proved efficient
despite weather and Indians

Strict regulations now govern the use of ponies in coal mines

1,000 a year, and in a year or so there will be virtually none left. Larger ponies up to 14 hands are used mostly in the Midlands and Wales where the seams are thick, the smaller animals working in the thinner seams of the north. Working in a coal mine is not an ideal existence for a pony, or for a man, but animals are creatures of habit and it is unlikely that pit ponies consciously miss life above ground. Animals are concerned with the treatment they receive, and here pit ponies are better off than some that work beneath open skies. They have been rigidly protected for years by the Coal Mines Act. Only geldings or entires more than four years old may be used, and, except in emergencies they only work two shifts or seven-and-a-quarter hours in twenty-four. Ponies no longer draw coal tubs, but bring required supplies on light trucks. Their stalls must be of adequate size, lime-washed in green to obviate glare, and ventilated by intakes of fresh air. Food is rendered dustproof, there is one keeper to every fifteen ponies and an inspector, obligatory on every pit, has the oversight of ponies as his special charge. Each pony has a yearly veterinary examination in addition to routine veterinary attention. There also exists that indefinable partnership that grows between a man and his horse. The miners are immensely proud of their ponies, taking such good care of them that even twenty-year-olds are often in excellent working condition. When pensioned off, they retire to homes of rest or, on condition there is no work attached, to good private homes approved by the R.S.P.C.A. The fate of the younger ponies made redundant by

44

automation is not so easy, although the Coal Board and various societies do their best to ensure their future.

Thousands of small, hardy ponies, in appearance not far removed from their remote ancestors, do every kind of work in Mongolia and in many districts of the Chinese Republic. In Greece, those still used on the farms and as pack ponies in the Peloponnese sometimes sport head collars of the same pattern as was customary 1,000 years before Christ. There are decorative Haflingers, chestnuts with cream manes and tails and decked out in colourful harness and jingling bells, drawing sleighs around the Swiss mountain resorts. When the snow melts they revert to drawing strange-looking wheeled vehicles, even more old-fashioned than the pony-drawn buggies providing transport on the island of Sark.

Ponies are used for all kinds of harness work in Malta and are often driven without a bit

There are ponies at work everywhere under the hot sun and blue skies of Malta – on the farms, taking produce to market, or harnessed to little 'gay carts' carrying everything from bread to petrol around the streets of Maltese towns and villages. Even among the bustle of the fast growing city of Cape Town in South Africa, the whining horn of the fish-man can still be heard, and the clip-clop of his shaggy pony's hooves.

In London there are still coster ponies to be seen, rattling along through the near empty streets of early morning, on their way to or from the borough markets. One general dealer alone hires out thirty-four ponies from his Fulham stables, and they can be seen plodding their routes, carts filled with fire-wood, greengroceries or flowers, or occasionally standing patiently at a parking meter. Many London coster ponies have their annual day of glory when, decked up to the nines, they are driven in the Harness Horse Parade in Regents Park. Billy, a chestnut pony, competed in the Coster's Turnout until he retired twenty-nine years old, and also appeared in the Parade of Personalities at the Horse of the Year Show with his wonderfully decorated greengrocery cart.

Because the islands of Indonesia have few roads, and grazing is too sparse to support full-size horses, life there continues to revolve around hundreds of indispensable ponies. They gallop flat out carrying local chieftains in the popular sport of lance throwing and trot indefatigably through the tropical heat, drawing the two-wheeled 'sados' that provide much of Java's transport. They trudge along the sands on the island of Bali, supporting large baskets slung on either side of the high saddle, to carry the stones collected for wall building. The prized ponies of Sumba, each with a small boy on their back, stamp and wiggle to the rhythm of tom-toms, jingling the bells on their legs and performing to their owners' directions imparted by lunge-rope. Further east on Timor, the sturdy little ponies are ridden without saddles or bits for working

The Lesotho police are the only fully mounted force in the world, riding sturdy countrybred ponies

cattle, and the same strain is also found in Australia.

Baby Doll is an Australian pony, but not of Timor blood. She was in fact a mistake, the surprising result of turning out a pony mare as company for the station horse, a Thoroughbred and supposed gelding. Baby Doll stands 13·3 hands high, has the general appearance of a miniature quarter horse, and the bone and stamina to make light work of thirty pounds of stock saddle, and twelve stones of Chilla Seeney – the top Australian rodeo rider who owns her.

This pony is a character. She loves to have her stomach tickled, even delaying Chilla's exit from the yard until he has obliged. She never fails to come to a whistle, unless of course there is an audience waiting to appraise this demonstration of obedience.

Schooled entirely by her owner, Baby Doll is easily fast enough to keep level with a steer, while Chilla leaps from her back to catch the beast by its horns and throw it in bull-dogging competitions. In roping contests, when the horse takes the strain, keeping the rope taut to prevent the thrown steer from rising, Baby Doll uses courage and intelligence to compensate for her lack of weight.

Each year the increasing tourist and holiday trade provides more work for ponies. When passengers break their cruise to go ashore at Haiti, among other perhaps more sophisticated delights the island can supply over 100 sure-footed ponies, willing to transport visitors over the rocky ground to the Citadel Henri Christophe, and the Sans Souci Palace. For a small amount you can also hire a quiet pony to carry you in company up through the flat-topped pine trees of Troodos in Cyprus, and 5,500 feet to the top of Chionistra or 'Mount Olympus'. This must be the cheapest and most enjoyable method of attaining the home of the gods!

Trekking derives from the Africaans 'trek', meaning to travel or migrate, especially by ox-wagon. In its modern form trekking came into being after the Second World War. Perhaps it owed part of its rapid popularity to an unconscious need to get away from the mechanically propelled horrors of war, to creatures of flesh and blood and the beauty and silence of countryside inaccessible to motor vehicles.

Trekking caters for all tastes and grades of experienced or would-be horsemen. You can tour on spirited horses through the beauties of Spain and Portugal, or across the wide puszta of Hungary, and Haflinger ponies will take you safely up and down the flower-decked slopes of Tyrolean mountains. Although today's Basuto ponies may not have the quality of their famous predecessors, you will find no more faithful conveyance for the precipitous, rocky paths of the Drakensberg mountains. They will carry you past tumbling waterfalls and green valleys far below, with antelope springing from beside the track and glimpses of klipspringers and

dassies basking in the sun, to the top of the escarpment – where a clear day reveals the sparkle of the Indian Ocean eighty miles away, and to the north the rolling hills of Zululand.

In Iceland, travel by pony is the only way to take in all the impressive natural wonders of the country. Based on hotels, you can ride daily, or venture further afield while your baggage is sent on by car. The attractive native ponies will take you happily across fields of moss-covered lava to see volcanic craters, geysers that spurt and hots springs that foam, and then will graze quietly beside some tranquil lake while you eat your lunch.

In Britain there are hundreds of trekking centres from which to make a choice. Some cater only for adults, some for children, but the majority make provision for all the family, grading out the

A tumbling mountain stream provides welcome refreshment for these trekkers' ponies

Puff takes a break from filming for a television series in his studio stable

riders so that the more experienced go further afield, and the novices can make expeditions within their capabilities. There are centres where the ponies are exploited by unscrupulous people intent solely on making money, but these would cease to flourish if trekkers patronized only those places approved by the Ponies of Britain Club.

The trekker's normal pace is a walk, and since most native ponies can carry adult riders at slow speeds and all the British breeds are sure-footed with an inbuilt hardiness and endurance, most centres gladly utilize the ponies of their own locality. You can visit the New Forest where all-purpose ponies, renowned for their good temper and easy paces, will carry you among the age-old trees of the forest or across the open heaths where they were born. Alternatively you can explore the dim distances of Dartmoor and Exmoor, on ponies that are smaller but equally sturdy, being able to carry adults with ease.

Among the mountains of Wales trekking centres exist to suit all tastes, with cat-footed ponies ranging from the lovely Welsh Mountain, to the Cob which combines fiery good-looks with an easy temperament. There are free-striding Fell and weight-carrying Dales ponies, trekking among the untamed hills and valleys of the north. The Highland ponies add to the pleasure of riding around the heights and through the heather surrounding their native Aviemore. If you fancy the mountains of Mourne, or a track through the woods at Rostrevor, what better mount than a

Connemara pony, Ireland's native breed?

Ponies are not allowed on the beach at Auckland, or on many others in New Zealand, but there are plenty of places in the world where ponies do ply for seasonal trade beside the sea. Some of these animals are in poor condition, or immature, and a proportion of the riders are as thoughtless and ignorant as some of the animals' owners. However, the majority of beach ponies are well cared for. Usually the work entails a short trip there and back for a shilling or so, but the Morecambe beach ponies do a more adventurous trek, way out to the open sandy reaches away from the crowds.

On the expanses of sand at Arromanches in Normandy sleek little Shetlands from a herd bred specially for the work, share the giving of rides with an Anglo-Arab and several larger ponies, grey, and bay, and the piebald and skewbald that is the traditional colouring of Ireland's gypsy ponies.

Nowadays many of the so-called gypsies are not of true Romany blood, but merely feckless folk who take to the road when all else fails. Romanies were the traditional horse-dealers of the world, but now even they mostly travel by dilapidated lorry rather than the gay, horse-drawn caravans of former days. Yet in the vicinity of many a roadside camping site, away from the litter of vehicles, you can often see gypsy horses and ponies tethered in the old manner by a collar round the neck, grazing the mixed herbage of the hedgerows that ensures their good condition.

The world changes, and people still predict the disappearance of ponies from the working scene. But ponies, like most things, adapt, and if one form of work disappears then another will soon take its place. For example, ponies may not today spank along the roads drawing tradesmen's traps, but they do sometimes work in television studios. Tinker, small, furry and as attractive as his youthful owner, was to appear in a children's series on looking after ponies, shown on Brisbane television. The rehearsal had not been an unqualified success, but it was felt that Tinker, imperturbable and sweet, was certain to be a winner. The attractive pair, pony and small boy, were the admiration of all concerned until the cameras started whirring. Then Tinker succumbed to stage fright, turned his furry rump to the camera, and refused to be reversed.

Tinker's performance, which in fact proved very popular, was not the polished affair staged by Puff, a small grey pony that combined television appearances with his more regular occupation of teaching children to ride at a school near London. This pony was the star of a television series covering basic pony management during 1969. From first to last, whether under the bright, hot studio lights, among the inevitable tangle of cables, or resting between performances, Puff behaved with the reliable composure of an old stage trouper.

Gypsies, like Indians, have always been fond of 'coloured' ponies or 'paints' as they are called in the USA

Below
Ponies are indispensable for gather-
ing sheep on Exmoor

Bottom
Ponies are ideal for taking riders of
all ages and riding standards out
from trekking centres into the heart
of unspoilt countryside

*Trekkers riding along the moonlight
trail at Otago, New Zealand*

It is necessary to cull the herds of wild deer in Scotland to keep their numbers within bounds and a Highland pony is strong enough to carry the heavy carcass of a stag

Sometimes this pony takes his owner
to a meet in his farming float, and
then they join the hunt

*Beach ponies are popular on the
continent as well as in England*

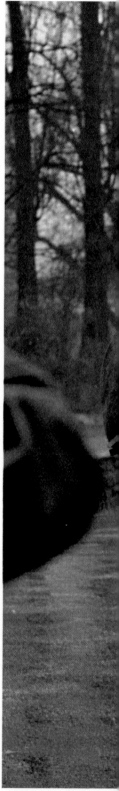

This diminutive Shetland in Germany may be smaller than its horse companion but is as willing to draw loads suitable for its size

Few people go to work like this nowadays but there is at least one doctor who prefers ponies to cars

Driving and racing

Despite his sullen expression, the small bay pony with black harness attaching him to a solid little governess-cart, made up an attractive turn-out. Like most women I lose my head at sales, and when lot 33 came spanking into the ring I refused to listen to the whisperings of commonsense – that the sparkling performance put up by the pony was due almost entirely to the skill and showmanship of the dealer driving him.

Inevitably, Japhet was not a success. Immature and scarcely broken, his innate obstinacy was matched by my total inexperience in driving, and the hours we took to get anywhere made expeditions scarcely worthwhile. The only time Japhet really moved was when he dived unexpectedly through some gateway, to rattle up to an unknown front-door despite my frantic efforts to turn and make an unobtrusive getaway.

Eventually Japhet departed, and some demon inspired me to have Blaze broken to harness. He was the right dimensions for the cart and gear, but few animals could be less suitable for a nervous novice to drive than our peppery pony, with his wary, bulging eyes and penchant for having highstrikes when things did not go according to plan.

Blaze condescended to stand for hitching up, so long as the operation was not protracted, but the only way to get aboard was to head him up the steep hill on which we live, and take a leap into the back of the cart from a running start. My husband, less horse-minded but with more nerve and unexpected driving ability, appreciated the pony's speedy, untiring trot, and remained relatively unmoved when any check to our progress sent Blaze straight up on to his hind legs. After attending a meet of the local foxhounds, our small pony's aspirations to join the hunt, governess-cart and all, inspired him to bring us the eight miles home in thirty-five minutes – but it was as well that our route was unimpeded. My driving career ended outside the village store, on the day Blaze kicked himself free of cart and harness, and subsequently reverted to what he considered his job in life – a riding pony.

Ponies of roughly Dartmoor size drew Boadicea's chariots, those successful fighting machines furnished with deadly knife-armoured wheels, but small animls would have been of little use for the deep-rutted roads and cumbersome vehicles of the Middle Ages. With the advent of hard road surfaces ponies became indispensable for tradesmen, and from Victorian times up to the First World War were fashionable for conveying ladies in elegant pony-chaises, and transporting the children with their governess – in the deep, safe 'tub' that was named after her.

Motorized traffic sent most of the harness horses and ponies off the roads, until the restrictions of the Second World War brought out the gigs and dog-carts, the traps and buggies long forgotten in

59

Continental ponies seem to get as much amusement out of driving as their young owners

outhouses, and put riding cobs, children's ponies and hunters alike between the shafts. This new interest in driving survived the removal of petrol rationing, and was given impetus by the magnificent collection of coaches and carriages seen in 1953, as part of Queen Elizabeth II's coronation procession. Today, in Britain alone, an estimated 5,000 drivers take to the roads each weekend, and the British Driving Society has more than 1,000 members. Some people drive horses, but the majority trot along behind a miscellany of ponies, ranging from Shetlands and Welsh Mountains to New Forest and Fell.

Show harness classes are yearly becoming more popular. The American renaissance in driving is confined almost entirely to the show ring, and in Britain a spectacular, and sometimes hazardous

A pony and trap is as much fun in a driving class as on the road

driving test, twisting and turning in and out of obstacles against the clock, is being well received by both contestants and spectators.

When the deep snows of winter blanket the North American and Canadian countrysides, children living in rural areas have the fun of driving out in company, with their ponies harnessed up to sleighs, some of which are old enough to be dubbed antique. Other children ski behind their ponies, or utilize them for dragging home Christmas trees. They find the snow itself a useful asset to breaking ponies to harness, because if the animal makes off its run can be halted by a snow bank. Care has to be taken in the following spring however, for then a young pony broken to drawing a sleigh has to be carefully re-educated to the disturbing and unaccustomed sound of wheels immediately behind.

Driving is almost as popular as riding in Scandinavia

The most spectacular driving pony of all is a Hackney, a 14-hand miniature of the Hackney horse in its brilliant, breathtaking action, but with more pony characteristics in its appearance. The majority of Hackney ponies have a temperament to match their fiery looks, and nowadays they are mostly confined to the show ring where they are driven by experts.

Most willing and imperturbable ponies go well in harness although some breeds, like the Welsh and the New Forest, seem particularly suited. Mr Dean Bedford, an American from Maryland, drove a pair of Highland mares to a four-wheeled dog-cart with conspicuous success in several of the 1968 British Shows before shipping them to the USA. They were obtained for him by Miss Henschell of Aviemore. The small, hardy Shetlands are also ideal ponies to drive in harness and in fact this breed is popular with many people in Holland.

Driving is an art that can be enjoyed at almost any age. The winner of the Welsh Mountain pony harness class at the 'Royal Welsh' in 1969, was aged ninety-one. In the same year, at a parade staged by the Driving Society in between polo matches at Cirencester Park, one of the eye-catching turnouts was an 1880 Hampshire spring cart, drawn by a Welsh pony mare driven by a nine-year-old girl. Only a year or so ago one of the best known figures at Canadian shows was another little girl of the same age, who expertly handled a team of Shetlands.

Towards the end of the nineteenth century Strawberry Girl, a celebrated trotting pony of 13·2 hands, won numerous handicaps both under saddle and in harness – the latter a sport that is now only occasionally seen in England, in some parts of the north. Down in Hampshire they still hold real old-fashioned point-to-points, scampering over the rough going on open tracts of the New Forest. There are races of various lengths with special events for children, but whether the jockey is adult or child all the point-to-pointers are New Forest ponies.

In many parts of the world ponies have been ridden in races for centuries, and now pony harness racing is growing in popularity. Gotland ponies are raced this way in Sweden, or ridden by children in saddle racing. There is no age limit to the jockeys who ride 13-hand Iceland ponies in the 800 metre gallop at a race meeting in south Iceland, and no betting on the event either. When Australians first went 'racing mad', following the 1851 gold rush, pony racing became immensely popular. These meetings were held on tracks so rough that they were only fit for a goat to run on, and so dangerous that one was closed after several jockeys had been killed. A government decree soon after the beginning of the century, put an end to this and other unregistered racing.

The stout little Fjord pony belies his figure by good speeds on the

This attractive pair of Highland mares were winners at several English shows before being exported to the USA

The winner of the Welsh Mountain pony harness class at the Royal Welsh Show 1969

The field moving out to the start. These children are racing in honour of the Crown Prince's birthday at Tehran racecourse.

Adults sometimes drive ponies in American harness races

harness trotting tracks of Denmark. In the USA, where racing of trotting and pacing horses has long been a top sport, the pony version is comparatively new but rapidly growing in popularity. The majority of the drivers are amateurs, out to savour all the thrills and spills of the racetrack without being involved in the large sums of money that make horse tracks almost exclusively professional ground.

American harness racing ponies must not be more than 12·2 hands. Some races are restricted by time classifications, some by height limit, some are for square trotters, some for the newly emerged pacing ponies. There are races for ladies, for two or three-year-old ponies, and for different breeds such as miniature Hackneys, Welsh ponies, and Shetlands. The latter, with their speedy action and similarity in looks to a dwarf version of the American saddle horse, are very unlike the Shetlands of their native islands.

Approved pony racing tracks are a quarter-mile in circumference, but some racing takes place on the half-mile trotting tracks found on most country fairgrounds. The ponies dash around these tracks drawing pony sulkies, which consist of little more than a precarious seat for the driver, perched above a pair of wheels with long shafts meeting behind the seat.

The Ponies-of-the-Americas, known as P.O.A.s, add racing to their numerous accomplishments both in the USA and Canada,

although in 1969 there was only one of these ponies harness racing in Florida. They are very fast and at one time there were a number of saddle racing events for children. It was then decided that unless both child and pony were properly trained, racing was not a very good idea, and P.O.A. shows no longer feature racing as such. In Canada children compete with their P.O.A.s in harness racing, but when it comes to thrilling and hazardous contests such as pony chuck wagon and chariot racing, it is the fathers who take over from their offspring.

European aristocracy took to driving for pleasure and display during the sixteenth century. This seemingly harmless pastime was frowned on by the rulers, who feared that their noble military commanders might abandon horse riding, and with it their fitness to go to war. Nowadays the resurgence of interest in driving is another pointer to man's growing, if subconscious, awareness that he cannot live by machinery alone.

Despite my personal ineptitude with harness ponies, there are few things more pleasant than bowling along country lanes with only the 'shusssh' of wheels and 'clip-clop' of hooves to distract one from a leisured view of the beauty on the other side of the hedge-rows. Yearly more families are discovering that this is the answer to the agonizing moment when the youngest child outgrows the family pony.

Shetlands often compete in harness races in the USA, but these spirited and speedy little animals bear little resemblance to their Scottish island ancestors

Royal ponies

Queen Victoria enjoyed nothing better than exploring the hills surrounding Balmoral on one of her beloved ponies

Velasquez, court painter to Philip IV of Spain, depicted the Infante Balthasar Carlos sitting, with admirable aplomb, on what appears to be an attractive, plump pony performing a spectacular movement of haute école. When Elizabeth I of England delivered a rousing, anti-invasion oration to her subjects at Tilbury, only one small painting confirms the written records, that she was mounted on a quiet palfrey – one of those little saddle horses or ponies of about 14 hands, so popular in the Middle Ages for their comfortable pacing. All other portraits show the Queen riding a large, distinguished horse which the artist considered more suitable for the event. This was usually an animal on the lines of the imposing Neopolitan chargers that many British and European kings rode in public, after James I of England became the last sovereign to be mounted on a palfrey for a state occasion.

In the nineteenth century ponies were very popular with the royal ladies. The Princess Charlotte, who died in 1817, had a well-loved little grey mare called Spangle, and the original Windsor Greys, which used to convey Queen Victoria around the park at Windsor, were then scarcely more than ponies. As for Highland ponies, the intrepid Queen was never happier than when exploring her dear Scottish hillsides, carried by Fyvie or Locknagar, or another of this breed much favoured for their kind natures and cleverness in 'scrambling up over stones and everything, and never making a false step'.

The royal fondness for ponies was continued by Queen Victoria's grandson, the late King George V. He kept a smart little chestnut called Arabian Knight either in the Royal Mews at Buckingham Palace, to ride in London, or at Windsor Castle when the Court moved out there. He also had K. of K., a Basuto pony named after his donor, Lord Kitchener of Khartoum, but the love of his life was a grey Highland that lived on the royal estate at Sandringham.

Jock was a trained shooting pony that always carried the King to rendezvous with the beaters and keepers and their attendant labrador dogs and clumber spaniels, that were essential to his favourite sport. The King also used his grey pony to visit the tenants in their homes, or to ride around the estate inspecting the crops and the herd of big black cattle. In fact there were few days when George V was at Sandringham that he and Jock did not set out on one of the rides they both enjoyed so much. When the King died, his favourite pony by then white with age, was led in the slow funeral cortège that wound its way from Sandringham House.

Jock was as sweet natured and affectionate as another pony of the same name, the bronze-coloured part-Highland pony that Queen Elizabeth II, then Princess Elizabeth, rode at Balmoral as a teenager. But where the original Jock was as steady and quiet as any pony could be, his namesake remained full of lively high spirits

Prince Abdullah's Galiceno is one of a breed of pony that is growing in popularity with children in the USA

until the day of his death, at nearly thirty years old. This Jock, and a dun Norwegian pony called Hans, were looked after almost entirely by Princess Elizabeth and Princess Margaret during the wartime months they spent at Balmoral. There was a shortage of staff, and the future Queen and her sister had the fun and experience of grooming, feeding and saddling up their own ponies. They also had the unaccustomed and much appreciated freedom of riding, within reason, when and where they wished, escorted only by a policeman toiling along behind on a bicycle.

The Queen breeds a few Highland ponies at Balmoral today, together with the black Fell ponies first introduced on to the estate by her father, the late King George VI. Some of this young stock are sold as children's ponies, one or two that grow too large for stalking may go for trekking, but those of the right size and temperament are schooled for work during the shooting and stalking seasons.

Shetlands came into favour with royalty in recent years, at a time when many parents were beginning to appreciate them as first ponies, both for their lack of inches and their normally docile temperament. Some twenty years ago the Crown Prince of Sweden learned to ride on a Shetland, and the British King George VI gave his daughter Elizabeth a quiet little mare called Peggy, when the Princess was about four years old. There was also a notable character George, of roughly Shetland size and shape but of indeterminate ancestry, presented to the King and Queen when they visited a Durham coal mine.

George came straight from the pit-head to the range of royal stabling at Balmoral, where the young Princesses were delighted with their somewhat strange-looking pony. Unfortunately George's behaviour did not compensate for his lack of looks. He proved both obstinate and wilful, but however naughty, his antics could never match those of Dandy, an elegant pure white Shetland stallion that lives at the royal stud in Jordan.

Originally presented as a riding pony for Princess Alya, King Hussein's daughter by his first marriage, Dandy arrived prior to the present royal horsemaster's knowledgeable regime. The frightened constraint and uncomprehending treatment he received at the hands of inexperienced grooms, was guaranteed to make any high-spirited stallion both difficult and unreliable. Dandy remains beautifully cared for and as irrepressible as ever, kept as a kind of incorrigible stud pet. However, he can no longer indulge in the rough games he once obviously enjoyed with his boy groom, as Mahmoud is now in the Army.

No two Shetlands could be less alike in character than Dandy and Valkyrie, the small black mare presented to Queen Elizabeth II by the people of the Shetland Isles during a visit in 1960. The pony

During the summer holidays at Balmoral, Prince Andrew used to share his pony with his small cousin, Lord Linley

was destined as a mount for the Queen's second son, but as a toddler Prince Andrew was unimpressed. 'Don't like it! Take it away!' he announced on their introduction, but shortly changed his ideas to form what his mother aptly described as 'an amicable association' with his pony.

Valkyrie proved everything a first pony should be – co-operative with initial efforts at grooming and saddling; never restive when Prince Andrew and his younger cousin, Lord Linley, squabbled over who should oil her hooves or have first ride. Valkyrie made no demur at travelling to Scotland as railway freight, in a large packing case. She was as quiet and willing to scramble up the banks on to the lawns at Balmoral, as to stay close beside some noisy tractor that had caught the interest of her young rider. When the temptation to graze proved too strong and Prince Andrew tumbled over her head to land on the grass beside his pony, Valkyrie remained literally unmoved. Her good manners inspired her owner to the

When the Royal Family went to Balmoral, Valkyrie travelled up from Windsor by train as freight

point where he could accompany the Queen for short rides around the grounds at Balmoral, up and down the tree-lined grassy tracks at Sandringham, or among the beauties of the home park at Windsor.

School and other pursuits occupied Prince Andrew for a time after he outgrew Valkyrie, but interest in what Princess Anne refers to as his 'riding' revived when he insisted on taking over an elderly ex-polo pony of Prince Philip's. Zamba first appeared in this role at Balmoral in 1968. She is considerably too big for her new rider, but adapts her naturally quiet and co-operative nature to his requirements.

During the Scottish royal holiday in 1969, Prince Andrew's Zamba contributed to the clatter of hooves each morning that sounded either on the drive in front of the castle, or on the grey stone stable yard, as a cavalcade set out for the bridle paths leading off the estate on to the hill. Led by a girl groom, sometimes riding Pink Gin – the pony intended for Prince Andrew – would be Lord Linley, despite his youth a great one for speed, dashing along on his cream pony Buttercup; his sister, Lady Sarah, riding a small Fell called Tinker; and bringing up the rear, a groom on a bicycle leading Valkyrie's successor with Prince Edward. This is the admirable Mr Dinkum, an 11-hand Shetland cross, as co-operative and unperturbed when crawled over and under in the stable, as when ridden out in company.

In the Royal Danish Mews there was until recently a fuzzy little Scandinavian pony reminiscent of a rotund polar bear, and there are at least two, short-legged Shetlands in the Royal Iranian Stud outside Tehran. They are kept with spotted ponies from the Argentine, small donkeys of the type often ridden by priests in the south of Iran, and the rare, slender-legged Caspian stallion, Kuh-e-Nur, presented to the Crown Prince in 1968. There is also another Shetland, the elderly, shaggy white pony that the Princess Farahnez calls Persi.

On a warm, rose-scented day towards the end of October in 1966, a smart electric toy car appeared from among the gold and copper-tinted aspen trees that line the drive leading to the Saadabad Palace, the Shah's summer palace in the Shemiran district of Tehran. The car was driven round and expertly parked beside the imposing curve of stone steps leading to the palace entrance, and the small boy driver stepped out to unfurl his personal standard, that of His Royal Highness Reza Pahlavi, the Crown Prince of Iran, then six years old.

The impish little girl who scrambled out beside him, Princess Farahnez, two years her brother's junior, gave little heed to the car or its standard. She made directly for the royal grooms who were standing in the shade holding a collection of horses and ponies

*Prince Andrew, aged four, bringing
in his Shetland pony Valkyrie*

Persi, the little Shetland of Princess Farahnez, decked out in Royal Iranian trappings

Another royal Jock, seen in retirement, was ridden and looked after by the Queen, who was then Princess Elizabeth, during the time she was at Balmoral during the war

A groom at the Imperial Stud at Farahbad, Iran, has fun with a little Shetland

including two magnificent stallions to be ridden by the Shah, Shabro – a Turkoman horse for the Empress and the comparatively large skewbald Pelang for Prince Reza. Princess Farahnez had no eyes for these, her interest lay in the diminutive Persi, decked out in all the glory of Persian saddlery with trappings fashioned in crimson velvet. For the next half-hour, while the Shah showed off the paces of Azar and Khoshrow, and the Empress and Prince Reza rode in and out of the dappled shadows along the drive, Princess Farahnez chattered and laughed with pleasure as Persi carried her in pursuit of His Excellency and of the inexhaustible supply of titbits contained in his pockets.

Welsh ponies have often found a place in royal stables. When the Swedish Crown Prince outgrew his Shetland he rode a Welsh pony imported from Wales before taking on a lively Gotland, one of the Russ ponies indigenous to his country. Some of the various ponies that formed an integral part of Queen Elizabeth's and Princess Margaret's childhood were Welsh. Snowball, bought out of an Irish jaunting-car, was of the cobby Section C type, and the good-looking, well-mannered Greylight, the favourite of them all, was a Welsh Mountain pony. The Queen carried on this tradition with her own children. William, their first pony, came from Ireland but the next, Greensleeves, was a Welsh mare. By the time Prince Charles and Princess Anne were competing, with some success, in Pony Club shows and gymkhanas, they were sharing a much loved Welsh gelding called Bandit.

This cream-coloured pony had been bred and reared on the steep mountainsides of Wales, and his sure-footedness and physical toughness matched his delightful temperament and jumping prowess. It was a sad day when Bandit was outgrown and returned to his previous owners, and from then Prince Charles' riding enthusiasm waned, unlike that of his sister, until he became caught up in the thrills of playing polo.

Princess Anne however, acquired High Jinks – the pony with which she made her successful entry into eventing, and who, in the manner of versatile family ponies the world over, has become a much loved part of her life.

High Jinks is a dark brown Irish bred pony of about 14·2 hands that came over to England as an unbroken four-year-old, and was schooled at the same farm in Wiltshire where Bandit had received his training. His calm, co-operative nature responded to the experienced handling he was given. By the time, at six years old, he was chosen for Princess Anne and brought to Windsor, Jinks was an adaptable all-rounder, young and inexperienced, but just the type for a keen child to get along with. Both the Princess and her pony had a lot to learn about competing, but they quickly gained mutual confidence, since never diminished, and were happy to

Princess Anne, with Prince Edward as passenger, drove this charming pair of Haflinger ponies at a meet of the British Driving Society in Windsor Park. The ponies were presented to the Queen during her State Visit to Austria in 1969.

attempt most things. They also fully benefited from the instruction meted out to riders and ponies alike by the riding establishment that Princess Anne attended when she was at school – and where High Jinks spent most of the school terms.

The number of successes grew until Princess Anne came out of juvenile classes into the tough competitive world of adult horse trials. Now she competes as auspiciously with two good horses, but Jinks is far from forgotten. His competing days may be over, but the Princess rides him whenever she can spare the time, either at Windsor, along the trails and over the practice jumps in the wide acres of the park they both know so well, or across the good galloping of the stubble fields surrounding Sandringham, or on the estate at Balmoral, within the enclosure of heather clad hills.

Nowadays there are some new inhabitants among the royal ponies in Scotland, Franzi and Triska, the two chestnut, flaxen-maned Haflingers presented to the Queen when she paid a state visit to Austria in 1969. No doubt they initially received from Highland pony partisans the same criticisms of lack of size and suitability for stalking and shooting meted out long ago to the Fell ponies, introduced by King George VI. However, surefootedness and strength and not necessarily height, are the most important attributes of a good deer-carrying pony, and in these respects the two sturdy, attractive ponies from Austria can certainly hold their own. Used for generations among the mountains of their native Tyrol, Haflingers make nothing of carrying a load, however heavy, across the rough terrain of the Scottish moors.

*Prince Andrew still enjoys riding at
Balmoral, but he has long outgrown
Valkyrie*

**The two small sons of King Hussein
and Princess Muna, Prince Abdullah
and Prince Feisal, with their flaxen-
maned Galiceno ponies from Mexico**

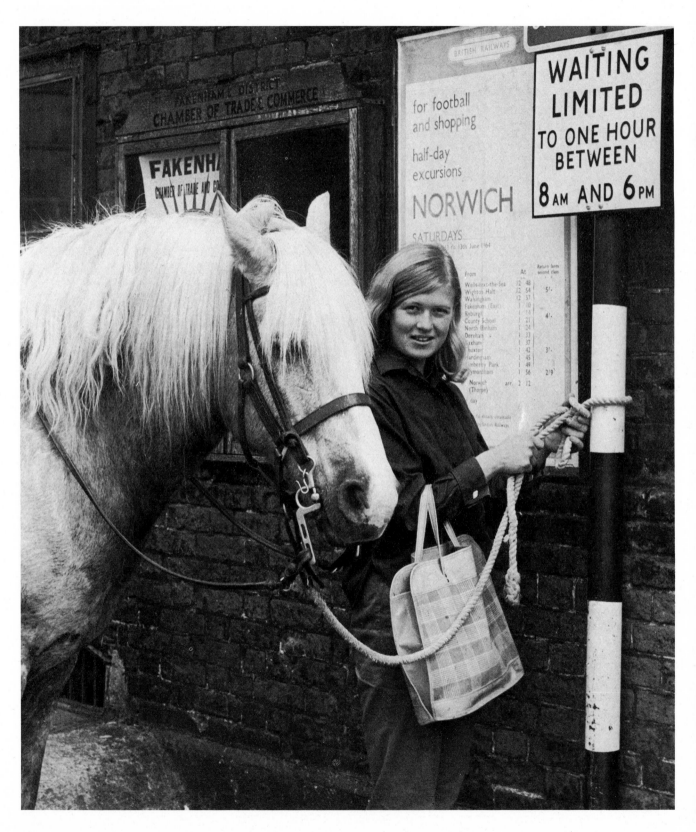

The family pony

Family ponies are those indispensable creatures of any, or no specific breed, but of the character and dimensions to cope with a family's riding requirements. They may lack beauty or blue blood, but all have their honoured place in countries where ponies are appreciated, and particularly in the British Isles.

A true family pony is hardy enough to live out, causing the minimum of work, and sufficiently versatile to take part willingly if not always at the highest level, in most equine activity. It combines physical toughness with an innately equable temperament, and grows wise in the ways of children and parents alike. When the children are grown up a family pony may perhaps be handed on to another lucky household, but it is seldom sold on the open market, for a good pony is worth its weight in gold.

At first glance the pony leaning over a dealer's gate some sixteen years ago, did not inspire the certainty that here was the prototype for all family ponies. The brown eye turned in our direction showed an expression both interested and mild, but gave no hint of the zany outlook imparted by the other, pale blue 'wall eye'. His white clown's face terminated in a pink muzzle, cut square at the base like a coal shovel. He was near black, stout, sturdy, and covered in a long, coarse winter coat. Clearly this animal did not rely on conventional good looks to attract a sale.

The dealer slipped a bit into the pony's mouth, clapped on a saddle and invited me to mount. I am no great horsewoman, and the day had not been without incident. There had been a giraffe-necked creature, carrying its head within an inch of my nose, that had carted me willy-nilly towards one of the dealer's fearsome jumps. There had also been a saddle flying through the stable door, closely followed by another prospective buy that immediately galloped away out of sight. Only a sense of responsibility towards our four young daughters persuaded me to get on to the wall-eyed pony's back, and out to the centre of the field.

Recollecting now the pearly milk teeth that were later to drop from the pony's mouth for a long time to come, there is no doubt he was younger than we were led to believe. Remembering the feeling he gave me that day, of two ends unattached in the middle where I was sitting, and judged by his total incomprehension of the aids, it seems probable he had been 'backed' only a few days previously. However, he listened amiably to what I had to say, made no effort to increase speed of his own accord, and for all his youth and ignorance, inspired me with confidence. When he did his best, ridden and urged on by the dealer's assistant to jump what was obviously the first fence in his life, my mind was almost made up. When he ambled up and down a main road, oblivious alike to the thundering traffic and the three small boys perched precariously on his broad back, the deal was clinched.

A versatile family pony should cope
happily with the hazards of a Pony
Club standard one-day event

We called him Twala, after the big, black, one-eyed Zulu king,
and he arrived home making those dismal sounds that dealers
ambiguously term an 'Irish cough'. The vet advised no riding and
prescribed two teaspoonfuls of cough mixture per day, and because
I am literally minded and Twala is Twala, he took the linctus
straight from the teaspoon, instead of sprinkled on his food in the
more conventional manner. The cough cleared eventually, and on
the day he was decreed fit for work Twala climbed a flight of steps
up a bank to supervise some fencing operations, slipped on the
return journey, wrenched his shoulder and went lame.

During the next few weeks our new pony became daily more
affectionate, following us around like an overpoweringly large dog,
and convinced us of something the years have since proved – that
he does not know how to kick. We also learned what can be a
mixed blessing to those without a stable, that Twala is an exceptionally good doer. By the time riding was at last on the programme, both his girth and youthful laziness had increased to an
alarming degree. It was hard work to get, and keep him out of first
gear, and the fourteen-year-old daughter who was at that time his
official rider, began to get disheartened. Trial and error, and indispensable, knowledgeable friends, taught us how to keep our pony's
figure within bounds, how to promote energy by correct feeding
and exercising, and how to utilize that energy by proper schooling.
Our mistakes were numerous, some of them horrific, but nothing
materially affected Twala's completely co-operative temperament.

Before very long he was fun to ride at Pony Club rallies, a patent
safety over small fences, and a certainty for at least one rosette at
local gymkhanas. He developed a permanent love of travel, diving
with eagerness into other people's trailers, and galumphing gaily
up the ramps of strange horseboxes if left unattended for a

Twala makes no bones about wearing unfamiliar western tack and bucking to order

Not all family ponies get the chance of working as an artist's model

moment. Twala's aptitude for going up and down flights of steps made sands below the sea wall always accessible, and no one could more enjoy the exhilaration of galloping in a cloud of spray, and leaping the breakwaters. Throughout the years there have been many big blood hunters happy to have the way over treacherous ground shown them by Twala, and he has always been amenable to galloping out in front with my daughters, or taking a considerably less ambitious position in the field when I have joined the hunt.

Twala has always loved people – not only those who fall for his 'poor starving pony' act and feed him most unsuitable but eagerly accepted gifts, ranging from ham sandwiches to ice lollies, but human beings as a race. He retains a special affection for his own 'family', often treating us to a high-pitched and ludicrous humming with excitement, at the mere thought of going for a ride.

It is now many years, and rosettes, since Twala won his first hunter trial, in a pairs class – galloping faultlessly over the fences stride for stride with his partner, an elderly and experienced cob, despite his unnerving resolve to turn and gaze throughout at his 'teacher' instead of where he was going. Musical baskets and potato races became a speciality, and he was usually placed in junior one-day events – although his rotund conformation filled most dressage judges with ill-concealed gloom. He has always jumped anything from wire to water, in hot blood or cold, only once being seriously discomposed by an unexpected encounter with a large plastic swan, floating on the muddy waters of an open ditch.

In show jumping Twala's style is effective, but uninspiring. He prefers to approach fences at a speed that disguises any apparent enthusiasm, gauging height with an accuracy born of sloth so that few are cleared by more than an inch or so. This method has a curious effect upon judges and spectators alike, making them raise one of their own legs high in the air in an unconscious effort to boost our pony over the top. Yet Twala's numerous successes include first in junior foxhunter and local jumping competitions, as well as a breathtaking and successful jump-off in a junior open – when only the tips of his ears were visible as he came into a five-foot wall.

Picnics and shopping expeditions can always include Twala because he will hitch up anywhere for any length of time. When tied in the garden, adjacent bonfires and lawn-mowing operations provide objects of calm interest. Alien stables hold no terrors, and nothing in the world puts him off his food. It is impossible not to catch our pony, but difficult to evade him when we are repairing fences and he insists on helping – by picking up the hammer or a tin of nails. Swimming in the sea plus rider is a favourite occupation

An ability to get on with other pets is another useful characteristic in a family pony

The sands at low tide are a good place for a trek

*True family ponies are prepared to
carry the family*

Most ponies enjoy a ride in the sea and some will gladly join their rider for a swim

– and when up-ended by a wave whilst being filmed for television, he was considerably less put out than the daughter astride him. Many years ago he came straight out of his field one summer dawn, to amble sixteen miles to Dover with his art student rider, model at the school all day and plod home again in the cool of the evening.

Twala has also acted as a photographic model for a book, demonstrating among other things, the use of cavaletti and lunging, and the jumping of anything from a wingless hurdle to a series of poles set at odd angles. The work took a day, and when it was discovered the camera was faulty, he gave an exact repeat of his performance on the next day even though it happened to be blowing a gale at the time.

When we made a television series on rough ponies our stud comprised four, Slingsby and Twala ridden by daughters Penny and Sue, the handsome The Magenpie for Tessa, and our splendid Little Gent coping with Frances. For some reason never explained, I had only forty-eight hours notice of the camera team's imminent arrival for three days work. This meant extricating the two youngest from a couple of irate headmistresses, placating the Art School sufficiently to release Sue and worst of all, appropriating Penny from a job. It meant borrowing a suitable estate and amenities from some long-suffering friends, and catching four muddy ponies, all singularly obstreperous after being on holiday since the beginning of term. With two stalwart lady riders I trotted them around the lanes for hours in an effort to stop them bucking.

My script and knowledge of television production were non-existent. The camera team had never before been in close contact

with ponies, and by the end obviously hoped they never would be again. Because the series had to be authentic, we put in everything – with one exception. When Sue, dashing for shelter from a rainstorm, inadvertently rode Twala on to the rotted cover of a car-inspection pit in the yard, it gave way and the pony fell in, his bulk occupying exactly the tomb-like hole. It was a moment of high drama and awful anxiety, and Twala was the only calm one among us, placidly chewing the straw we were frantically trying to pack beneath him. By the time we freed him with the aid of a rope and an old fashioned groom who sat on Twala's head at the appropriate moment, the situation was too tense for any filming.

Sue and Twala were filmed without saddle or bridle and quite unrehearsed, jumping a hand-held pole, and including the hefty buck of joie de vivre he produced the other side. There were shots of the well-schooled Magenpie, supposedly demonstrating the calm training of a pony on the lunge, surprising us, and his rider, by putting on a rodeo instead. There were long-range shots of Gent's rotund rear when unexpectedly camera shy, he carted a protesting Frances into a nearby copse instead of waiting to exhibit dismounting and unsaddling. The final results produced six episodes at weekly intervals, some cash, and a lot of fun.

Now Twala's young riders are scattered around the world and he is semi-retired, but always eager to go riding with anyone who has the time. His pleasure was apparent when two of my daughters returned home together to enter for a pairs class at a local show, brought Twala straight from his field and commandeered Slingsby from the riding school where he earns his keep.

*On a hot day, a shady woodland ride
is particularly enjoyable*

*A family pony worth his salt will
tackle anything to please the family*

Foals are lovely but they take a long time to grow into a suitable pony for a novice child

Most family ponies live out like this one in Australia, but they still need careful grooming

The ponies tally in size, colour and markings, if not in shape, and the sisters were dressed exactly alike, even to their buttonholes. They won first prize, and only we realized that Twala's zest and happiness at competing once more made him match his grass-fed bulk stride for stride with the stabled, corned-up Slingsby. Only we knew how much his neatly trimmed tail and plaited mane owed to a last minute and scandalous use of nail scissors – and luckily no one spotted the liberal application of black boot-polish that covered the bare patches on his rump, where he had rubbed against a tree.

At the moment Twala's forte is to make appearances at local fêtes, accoutred in the western saddle and bitless Hackamore that Frances brought back from Canada, to offset her own authentic stetson and chaps. He gives rides, and has learned to buck to order if required. His 'family' still ride him whenever they return, he still goes sea bathing, and my life continues to revolve around him. Now an advertizing company are showing interest in our pony's amiable ability to do anything required of him. Maybe in the future a whole range of products will be promoted by a bulky pony with a shovel-shaped muzzle and a zany wall-eye, who will appear on our television screens with regular monotony.

*Whiskers will go through water
without fuss – a great help when it
comes to competing*

Like all good ponies Whiskers is traffic proof and his rider knows the correct hand signals

Competing is all in a day's work

Looking after ponies

Good, clean tack spells comfort and safety for pony and rider

Ponies are delightful, sensitive animals, but they are not pets in the accepted sense of the word. Loving a pony is not enough. You also have to know how to look after and master a creature many times stronger than yourself; and to do this you must be capable of understanding how your pony's mind works, as well as learning its basic physical requirements.

For thousands of years horses, ponies and their donkey relatives provided the only means of transport. They were the indispensable working partners of mankind. Everyday life depended on their good health and co-operation, so that good horse and pony management came to be of maximum importance. Even when motorized transport became widespread and horses and ponies became associated mainly with sport and relaxation, there was still a tradition of keeping horses, a literal 'horse sense', alive in most of those families who owned them. In the British Isles it is only lately that a generation has grown up without this experience to guide it, and these people and their children are often the pony owners of today.

The majority of families that acquire ponies do so through genuine interest, but there are parents who give in to the pleas of children more horse-mad than pony-wise, without first giving due thought to the responsibilities involved. There are unfortunately just a few with a good income but lacking an understanding of animals, who look on a pony as a status symbol. Deliberate cruelty is happily rare, but many ponies suffer through ignorance, or from the mistaken belief that children are capable of looking after ponies without adult supervision. Unlike a bicycle, a pony cannot be parked and forgotten until it is next needed.

Obedient, well-schooled ponies are a joy to ride, but they do not automatically remain well trained in the hands of a complete beginner. Before you acquire a pony of your own the rudiments of correct riding, schooling and management at least should be learned from the kind of knowledgeable people who run good riding schools.

Because mannered ponies in the prime of life are expensive, some people imagine it an economy to buy a young animal. They do not realize that immature ponies under four years old, are unfit both physically and mentally for anything but the lightest work, and that all young ponies are suitable only for experienced riders to train. Young ponies do not grow up happily with either young children or novices, and too often this type of association results in a frightened child with no wish to ride again, and a spoilt pony, sold downhill through no fault of its own. First ponies should be steady but willing, and completely reliable under all circumstances and in all types of traffic. This is essential nowadays for every riding and driving animal. Because ponies often have a working

So long as you are not rough your pony will make no trouble about being bridled

Top class show and jumping ponies usually need to be stabled, but it does make more work

life of around twenty years, a kind old pony that is sound and knows its job is usually a good buy for a novice child.

In Australia and New Zealand ponies live out all the year round. In countries with extremes of temperature like that of Canada and North America, ponies either live in during the winter or shelter is provided at night. In Britain, ponies are happier and healthier living out, at least partially.

In the wild a pony would graze large areas of relatively poor pasture containing a variety of herbs and grasses. He therefore needs not less than two acres of average mixed grazing, or a series of smaller plots to which he can be moved in turn. A rich clover lea, suitable for cows, will make a pony grossly fat and susceptible to laminitis, a painful foot fever. Yew and laburnum trees are fatal, and ragwort and horsetail are both poisonous – and more likely to be eaten if cut and left in the field. In small areas droppings should be removed frequently to prevent the pasture becoming 'horse sick'.

All fencing should be strong, and high enough to discourage jumping. After one successful escape from his field your pony will be keen to repeat his accomplishment. Adequate shelter from the prevailing wind, for example a thick hedge, the side of a house, or preferably an open shed, is essential. Ponies hate flies and wind-driven rain, but do not mind dry cold. Some ponies live out even in the sub-zero temperature of a Canadian winter, thriving in deep snow as long as they have plenty to eat and the shelter of an open barn if required.

Correct feeding depends on your pony's size, age, temperament and breeding, the work he is expected to do and your own capabilities as a rider. Unless a hot summer burns up the pasture, native-bred ponies normally keep sleek and well on grass only, from about the end of April to the middle of October. Then your pony will need about as much good hay each day as he will eat. It should be placed in a hay net and hung high enough to avoid tangling his feet. During the spring flush of grass many ponies get fat, and should have their grazing restricted.

If your pony is doing a lot of work or as you enter the field of competing and he has to be fitter than the purely grass fed, you may need to feed concentrates in addition to grass or hay. These can be in the traditional form of crushed oats with a little bran, or one of the brands of horse and pony cubes. Bruised barley is often successful but it is advisable to consult an expert. It is impossible to lay down hard and fast rules, but initially a pound of concentrate a day in two feeds is sufficient, increasing to between four and six pounds for a 14-hand pony until you reach the point where the pony copes easily with the work in hand, and is lively enough to suit your taste. Small ponies ridden by young children should not

Even the smallest rider can learn to groom his pony

Correct grooming not only improves your pony's looks, it is also essential to his health

Shoeing roughly every four weeks by a skilled blacksmith is essential to your pony's well being. The blacksmith's assistant cuts off the heads of the nails so that the old shoe can be pulled off with pincers. The blacksmith first tries the new shoe for size and then nails it into place. Finally the horn is trimmed and the nail heads smoothed.

be given concentrates. A constant supply of fresh water is essential, whether in the field or in a stable, and ponies should be fed at regular times.

Ponies out at grass are insulated from the wet and cold by the grease in their coats and so grooming should be confined to removing surface mud and brushing out manes and tails. All ponies need the attention of a blacksmith at least every six weeks, even if their shoes are not worn down. Neglecting a pony's feet can have him out of work for a long time.

Well-cared-for ponies seldom ail. The signs of good health are bright eyes and an interest in life, skin that moves easily across the ribs and does not appear 'hide-bound', and an obvious ability to cope easily with the required work. A listless appearance, dull staring coat, bony ribs (possibly hidden beneath a thick winter coat), and deep grooves down the quarters, may be due to many causes ranging from an infestation of worms to insufficient or incorrect food. The only sure and sensible way of finding out what is wrong is to send for the vet. Remember that if your pony 'points' a front leg, this is a danger sign that must be investigated, but resting a hind leg merely means that your pony is relaxing.

You can get your pony fully fit and in condition for competitions, by keeping him stabled, and by combining feeding of concentrates and hay with daily exercise and thorough grooming. If your pony has a large percentage of Thoroughbred or Arabian blood, he will probably have to be stabled in winter.

Stabled animals are normally clipped in winter to prevent sweating and to facilitate the grooming necessary for health and muscling up, and kept warm with a rug by day, with an extra blanket underneath for night-time. Stabled ponies enjoy going out in the field for a few hours if weather conditions allow but if they are clipped they must wear a New Zealand rug. This is made of waterproof canvas with a warm lining, and with special leg straps to keep it in place if the pony rolls.

A stabled pony usually means hard work and extra expense. He must be fed three times a day at regular hours, with the largest feed and bulk of the hay in the evening. He needs about two hours exercise a day, a minimum of half an hour's grooming, and his box must be thoroughly mucked out daily. Bedding can be of wheat straw, barley straw without prickles, wood shavings, sawdust, or peat – which is expensive. Deep litter saves work, but must be managed properly. Only the droppings are removed and fresh straw or shavings added to the thick bed, the generated heat then drying out the bedding. A fresh start is usually necessary after about three months.

Well fitting, supple tack is comfortable and safe for both rider and pony. It is advisable to buy the best you can afford and to keep

Exercises on the lunge give the rider a safe seat, independent of reins or stirrups, and are excellent practice for both rider and pony if carried out correctly

Most ponies 'blow themselves out' when first girthed, so remember to check your girth soon after you have mounted

101

Well-taught ponies stand still while you first find your stirrup, reach for the saddle and then hoist yourself on

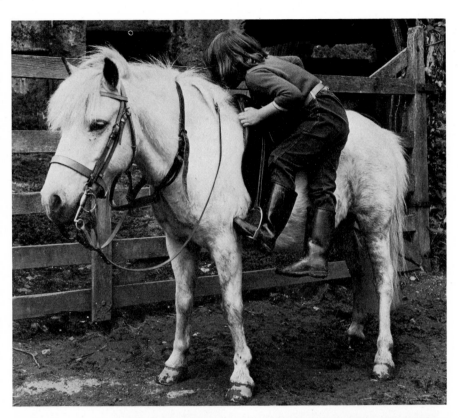

However, once on top you will not get anywhere if you have the reins too long

*If you teach your pony to jump at an
angle you will save time in speed
jumping competitions*

it clean by rubbing off mud and sweat after use, and dressing it with saddle soap. A modern general purpose saddle has a deep seat to help you sit in the correct position, and knee-rolls to help keep you there. A saddle must be clear of the pony's spine and withers, and must fit the pony as well as yourself. The bridle must allow room for the ears without cramping, with space for three fingers between throat-lash and gullet, and the same amount of space between the pony's nose and a cavasson nose-band. A dropped nose-band, used to give greater control, fits below the bit, lying in the chin-groove at the back, and on the bony part of the nose in front – but never low enough to impede the nostrils or breathing. Ponies are controlled by good schooling, and severe bits merely make them pull harder and resist because of pain. Some form of thick snaffle is a suitable bit, but if your pony hots up while jumping or hunting, try a vulcanite-mouth pelham until he settles down.

A pony has an excellent memory but limited intelligence, and is incapable of reasoning. Loud voices and sudden gestures will frighten and confuse him. Most ponies do their best to comply with their rider's wishes, but the aids – those firm and consistent signals of leg, hand and voice by which a rider converses with his pony – must be well understood by both of you. The reins are for keeping a light conversational contact with your pony's mouth and are not for holding on by.

Talk to your pony and make much of him. All ponies need affection, but also require sensible handling, and it is cruel to spoil them. If you give your pony too many titbits he may start nipping, especially if he is young, and unless checked can turn into a biter. If he is difficult to catch, coax him to you with a bucket of food; let him eat and then walk away from him. In this way he learns that your advent does not necessarily mean work. If your pony refuses to go one way on a ride circle him a few times until he consents to go on, or make him stand still until he is bored and eager to get going. If you give in to your pony, even in little ways, he will be twice as difficult the next time.

Never lose your temper or indulge in trials of strength – rather, learn your pony's limitations. If you ask him to jump a fence beyond his capabilities he may sensibly refuse or he may make the effort and hurt himself, and that is something he will not easily forget. Use your superior human intelligence, combined with consideration and tact, to be one jump ahead of your pony. He is completely dependent on you for his good manners and happiness, as well as for his physical needs, and the mutual trust and confidence that builds up between a happy, willing pony and his understanding and considerate owner provides a companionship that is more than worth while.

Mutual affection is essential but your pony must still know who is master

Competing and showing

Debbie Johnsey is only 11 years old and has a big future in the show jumping world

All over the world there are pony owners fully content just to ride around the countryside. They ask nothing more from this good companionship – and good luck to them. There are also those who would be happier riding their ponies in this way but who, spurred on by ambitious parents or the urging of friends, feel compelled to take part in the secretly feared publicity of shows and gymkhanas. This is a great pity because there are so many facets to owning a pony, and no two people get exactly the same pleasure from the relationship.

Once past the complete beginner's stage, the majority of children do want to compete against others and have the fun of trying to prove their own pony better than the next at something, whether it is in looks or at bending in and out of poles. Some are successful, some not, and all have to learn that even the best of ponies is not a machine, and is as liable to have an off day as its owner. Prizes and rosettes can be the cherished accolade to weeks of schooling, but they are not everything – the fun lies in taking part, and there are a variety of classes and contests devised to suit every type of pony and rider.

There are also horse and pony shows of all standards from the gymkhana races organized as part of a flower show in an English village, to the South African Rand Easter Show, second largest of its kind in the world, that runs annually for eleven days in Milner Park, Johannesburg. The Royal International Show that takes place each year in London, was originally conceived in Holland and first staged at Olympia in June 1907 – when the majority of the classes were for harness horses. In parts of Britain there are shows held specially for the local pony breed, and each year the National Pony Show and Ponies of Britain shows cater for all breeds and types, including working and utility ponies.

Modern show ponies are very expensive, yet few fortunes are made from actually breeding them. With some knowledge and a little luck it is not difficult to breed a good pony – and a filly in this category is more valuable than her colt counterpart – but it is a costly business, and the superlative animal that is the real money-spinner, is a rarity. The showing classes are the shop windows for different breeds and types. They are held primarily to help improve the overall quality, and all the entrants should be, as near as possible, models of the breeds they represent. Classes for specific British native pony breeds are included in many of the major shows, and this also occurs in Scandinavia, the USA, Canada and Australia. Dartmoor and Welsh ponies in particular sometimes hold their own in English show pony classes, but the majority of British show ponies are either bred from native mares crossed with Arabian or Thoroughbred blood, or are miniature Thoroughbreds in type. They are beautiful to look at and extravagant movers, but

A good entry for the pairs class

Show ponies are beautiful animals,
mostly with a percentage of
Thoroughbred blood. A show saddle
is cut straight to display the pony's
forehand.

Good show jumping comes with practice. This rider has a good leg position, her weight is off the pony's loins and the pony is jumping freely knowing that he will not be jabbed in the mouth.

often too hot in temperament for any but experienced riders. Australian and South African show ponies are seldom of this light-boned blood type, but often better suited by disposition and stamina to the various tasks required of them by their young riders.

In America and Canada the Pony-of-the-Americas has its own shows where, unlike the general rule in these countries, all riders must be children under sixteen years old. Many classes have been devised to exhibit and test the P.O.A.s' exceptional versatility. In addition to numerous 'in hand' showing classes for mostly young stock, there are performance classes like pleasure (for ponies well mannered at walk, trot and canter), western pleasure, Indian costume, trail or stock pony, and jumping competitions. Barrel racing figures as highly among the gymkhana events as the

The show jumping phase of a horse trial is non-competitive but will prove that your pony is both fit and versatile

bouncing pony contests in Australia, run over a series of low cavaletti.

Show jumping is prevalent in almost all horse-minded countries. Most ponies are natural jumpers whatever their breed or type, but some enjoy it more than others, and some have more courage and ability. Connemaras and other ponies originating from Ireland seem to have an inbred aptitude for the sport. No pony can jump his best unless he has a good rider, and pony and rider have mutual confidence in each other. If your pony is disinclined to tackle painted fences in the confines of the show ring, you may find him willing to cope with the more natural obstacles and greater freedom of a hunter trial course. Success and enjoyment here could encourage you to attempt the three phases, dressage, cross-country and low-fenced show jumping in a one-day event or horse trial. However, unless you are a member of a Pony Club you are unlikely to find one of these competitions run for children and ponies.

Trail riding is very popular in the USA, Canada and Australia, and rapidly becoming so in the British Isles. These competitions are not races as such, but sometimes gruelling tests of fitness and good horse and pony management. Where the trail leads over mountainous and rough country, ponies often have the advantage over horses, although they obviously cannot compete in the lengthy trails specifically designed for the larger animal. The

British Pony Club organizes trail rides for its members, and in the United States many trails are arranged for P.O.A.s only – a form of competition well suited to these tough, willing little ponies.

Whatever class or event you and your pony take part in, success is unlikely to come your way without a lot of hard work and patient schooling. Whether your pony is a show animal, or merely the family pony you are riding in musical baskets, the more willing, supple and obedient he is, the better your performance will be.

Showing is an art in itself, although it is easier to learn how to exhibit breeding or young stock 'in hand', than to exhibit a show pony under saddle. Whatever the class, the pony must be as well turned out as possible, and the rider or handler neatly and suitably dressed. The object of showing your pony is to make him present himself to advantage, and to attract the judges' and spectators' attention to the animal, but not to yourself. If you are showing your pony 'in hand', he should have been accustomed from the earliest days to being handled, to wearing a foal-slip and leading quietly, and to meeting people other than yourself. Teach him to stand out properly – the knowledge that a hand near your pocket could mean a pony cube will make him look alert – and to stand still, even when you move away a few feet in order to give the judge a good, uninterrupted view.

A pony shown under saddle has to be in show condition, adequately muscled, well covered without being fat, and suffi-

Hunter trials take one across country – good fun for pony and rider

New Forest ponies competing in a 30-mile long distance ride – not a race, but a test of fitness for both pony and rider

A nice stamp of pony for any young competitor

There are special classes for native breeds of pony. This is a fine Fell shown by an adult.

ciently on his toes to look attractive without losing his manners. The state of fitness required is not easy to achieve, and different from the hard fitness required for show jumping, eventing and trail riding. Good condition is attained by a judicious mixture of correct feeding, exercise and grooming, and since the requirements of ponies vary considerably, the art of achieving fitness is not learned in a day.

However well your pony jumps you are not going to be successful for long unless he is obedient. A natural jumper may cart his rider round a course or two, but unless he is under control and willing to combine courage and ability with his rider's wishes, the performance will owe more to good luck than good judgment – and this is not enough for the high standards of modern juvenile show jumping. Your pony must respond to your aids, conveyed by seat, legs and hands, so that he comes into his jumps smoothly and with plenty of impulsion, but willing to check speed or take off when required. On the rider's part there is a great deal more to this

Leading rein classes are for young riders and quiet little ponies

There is an art in showing a pony in hand and this Welsh Mountain stallion is exhibiting his beauty and paces to the best advantage

sport than the ability to stay seated over fences. You have to learn how to judge the distance between jumps, the best angle for coming correctly into the next obstacle, how to tackle an upright fence without getting under it, the extra push needed for a spread and the correct number of strides between the components of a combination jump. The most important rule of all is to get your heart over first, because a pony always senses and responds to any doubts or hesitations of his rider.

The largest proportion of a jumper's schooling takes place on the ground, and you should ride your pony at the trot in large circles to either hand to supple him, teach him to change direction with the lightest pressure of leg and rein, and to slow or push on calmly when you ask him. If you overjump your pony, particularly over the same old practice fences, he will soon tire of the game. If you put the fences up and up to see how high he can get, he will eventually reach his limit and stop – you have then 'overfaced' him, which is the first dent in his confidence. Increase the spread rather than the height and vary the form of the jump. Almost any obstacle from a fallen tree trunk to a wheelbarrow makes a jump – so long as it is not beyond your pony's capabilities, and not potentially dangerous. Get into the habit of popping over anything

Young riders and their ponies competing at a New Zealand show

jumpable when out on a ride. This makes jumping fun for your pony, and helps with all kinds of competitive jumping whether over show fences or across country.

Unlike British ponies which are schooled and ridden much more on the bit, those in the USA and many other countries are ridden with a comparatively low head carriage and loose rein – a method which often produces well-balanced animals and calmly competent jumpers. These ponies are taught to move away from the rein pressed against their neck and this is a great aid in gymkhana events. It also makes unnecessary the ugly yanking of ponies' mouths, that sometimes occurs in the heat of the moment to mar events in Britain.

Whatever form of competing you undertake, it should be enjoyable to both you and your pony. If he has confidence in you he will do his best, and there will be many times when your pony's cleverness makes up for your own lack of experience. You cannot ask for more from a partner and you should give him thought and consideration in return. Accept when he has had enough, put his well-being above your own ambitions and if the day does not work out according to plan, you must realize that it is just as likely to be your fault as your pony's.

An unusual but worthwhile class for parent and child seen at the Sydney Royal Easter Show

At some of the larger shows, ponies are still exhibited under side saddle

Pony Clubs

In the distance a lion was coughing, the distinctive sound still too far off to cause the picketed ponies more evident unease than a to and fro flicking of their ears. However, the branch chairman in charge of that particular Pony Club camp crossed his fingers. Cantering unexpectedly into a herd of giraffe that morning had created quite enough turmoil and excitement among children, ponies, and the elegant giraffes themselves, without the additional problem of a lion prowling around at night.

An enthusiasm for camping was born among the ten Pony Clubs affiliated to the Horse Society of Kenya some years ago, when the members of the Gilgil branch were taken on adventurous mounted treks, carrying their own gear on pack ponies. Now annual camps are increasingly popular and the chosen sites are always as far from human habitation as is compatible with ensuring supplies. The Molo Hunt and Kipkabus branches have made exciting and much appreciated mounted safaris through sun-drenched, varied tracts of country up to around 13,000 feet, just below the snow-line on Mount Kenya.

The chief hazard to Pony Club camping in Singapore is not lions, but the climate. This thriving branch usually rides at either the Polo Club or the Bakit Timah Saddle Club, most activities commencing at six o'clock in the morning to defeat the humid heat. In 1968, for the first time, the children camped at the Singapore Turf Club, where they appreciated sleeping in the jockeys' and stewards' inquiry rooms, with the added luxury of air conditioning and abundant ice. The ponies were in clover too. They were in the overall charge of their District Commissioner, who is also veterinary surgeon to the Turf Club, and occupied one of the saddling rings. The whole arrangement gave the children the opportunity to learn stable management – valuable experience even in a country where grooms are almost universal.

Some members of the Singapore Pony Club ride horses, but there are at least twenty genuine ponies, either sturdy utility types up to 14 hands and imported from Australia, or the smaller 'Borneo' ponies that are indigenous to Sumatra. These are exceptionally tough little creatures, very like cave drawings of the early horse, with sometimes rather nasty natures. All the animals thrive on good food and a variety of exercise. They include working rallies with contesting gymkhanas, hunter trials, Prix Caprilli tests and one-day events; play polo on occasions, and have been known to win a dressage competition only a couple of weeks before acquitting themselves courageously on the racecourse.

Many children belonging to the forty-two branches of the Canadian Pony Club ride horses, often cast-off racehorses, in preference to ponies. This trend, apparent in many countries, is partly due in this case to the fact that children are not graded for

Chinese members at a Singapore Pony Club camp taking part in a mounted game

showing in Canada – and a seven-year-old can show a 16-hand hunter if he has the inclination and the ability. The old prejudice against ponies is yearly growing less, and there are now numbers of Ponies-of-the-Americas, Welsh, Highland, and more recently introduced Connemara and New Forest ponies taking part in Pony Club activities. A few Canadian branches cater for children who ride 'western', adjusting the standard 'Grade C' Pony Club test for riders with stock saddles, nearly straight legs, and horses and ponies schooled to neck-rein.

In England the Pony Club functions only during school holidays. In Canada most branches continue all the year round; but unless there is an indoor arena, riding is replaced during the bitterly cold winter months by stable management and visits to studs, veterinary colleges and the like. The Dominion is divided into seven Pony Club regions for administrative purposes, but the vast distances involved make it difficult to transport riders and their mounts to compete in inter-branch and inter-regional events. A Canadian team however, is sent annually to the inter-Pacific Exchange with the USA, Australia, New Zealand, Japan, and the United Kingdom.

Some American Pony Club members ride ponies, but horses are the more general rule, and little thought is given to size of mount. Official reports always refer to the 'horses', but the declared goal of the Club is 'to produce thoroughly happy, comfortable horsemen, riding across natural country with complete confidence and perfect balance, on a pony equally happy and free from pain or bewilderment'. Founded in 1953, the American Pony Club has 177 branches spread throughout nineteen regions, and caters for 7,000 children. The organization is adapted to the varying types of country and size of individual branches, and here again camping, combining instruction with fun, is proving a conspicuous success.

In the spring of 1939, a New Zealand mother was recalling a magazine article on the British Pony Club movement, as she watched her daughter ride across the wide stretches of the Heretaunga Plains in North Island. The child's obvious happiness in her pony whether out on the plains, among the foothills of the Havelock Range or beneath the poplars of the home paddocks, inspired her mother to found the first Pony Club in New Zealand. The idea was forced into abeyance by the Second World War, but the first rally of the Heretaunga Pony Club was eventually held in January 1945.

The early days provided plenty of problems, but potential material was not one of them. Petrol was still rationed, and at the time riding was no luxury for those living away from the towns but rather a way of life. The majority of country children rode their ponies to school daily. The difficulty was to convince parents of

*The Blenheim Pony Club in New
Zealand have a perfect setting and
perfect weather for their gymkhana*

An Australian member discovers that if his pony refuses it is probably as much his fault as his pony's

the possibility that modern methods of riding and schooling ponies could be better than those they had employed for years while playing polo, mustering, show jumping and hunting. They felt in no need of newfangled riding ideas, either for themselves or for their children. The modern seat meant little to the small boy who rode bareback seventeen miles to and from a rally; holding reins in two hands, thumbs uppermost and with a 'soft' feel of the pony's mouth, appeared superfluous to the young Maori who was used to cantering along the shore, his pony controlled by a small portion of halter. Broad bottoms were for sitting squarely on; it was comfortable to thrust one's legs forward as Dad had always done, and convenient for masking the pony's poor shoulder in a showing class. Furthermore, if reins could not be made into a good, tight 'bridge' across the withers, what else could a child hang on by?

Pony Club teaching is not dogmatic, there is more than one way of doing most things, the only claim is that the Club way is a good one. The children continued to come to rallies in increasing numbers. Instruction was sandwiched between mounted games and competitions, members were encouraged on their own merits, and they had fun. It also became apparent that a trained pony more often than not beat an untrained one, and that it was practically impossible to 'bend' at the trot with arms folded and with knotted reins, if you had not learned to use your legs correctly.

The children from the cities and towns of New Zealand have benefited almost more from the Pony Clubs than their country cousins. The depression of the 1930s up to the last war made riding almost impossible for urban dwellers, but the scene changed dramatically with the birth of the Pony Club.

Enthusiasts were undeterred by a shortage of mounts in the towns. They turned up at rallies with any old 'prad' that was faintly rideable, often tacked out with sacks or sheepskins for saddles or, in one case, the remnants of a goat-skin hearthrug. Riders wore what clothes they possessed, and the few with well-cut jodhpurs had no advantage over those with home-made breeches or patched jeans. Love of ponies and the will to ride was all that counted.

Blacksmiths, traffic and grazing have become increasingly difficult problems. The car hazard is now so bad that anxious parents often drive alongside their children riding to and from a rally. Some families contrive to buy a few acres of grazing out of town for their ponies; some manage to track down the last remaining costly and dwindling pasture within reach of a suburban club headquarters; others utilize several quarter-acre patches, tethering the pony and carrying water by bucket. Grazing is now very expensive and feeding and shoeing expenses add to the real sacrifices necessary to keep a pony, but parents and children alike find it well worth while. The country child may be the luckiest rider alive, able to keep his pony at hand and with the freedom of hills and plains to ride where he will, but there are few weekends when there is not some rally or competition within reach of town Pony Club members. From April to August, in many parts of the country, children and ponies can get out of town to join in a day's hunting, a sport enjoyed by nearly all New Zealand Pony Clubs.

Most Pony Club associates and older members graduate to horses, and many of these become well-known performers. This applies to New Zealand too, but it has been the ponies of all breeds, cross-breeds, shapes and sizes, that have made Pony Clubbing

As long as the rider is not too heavy, a small pony is much hardier for gymkhana games

Australian Pony Clubbers are always sure of good weather for their outdoor activities

Instruction at a working rally in New Zealand

Despite the many miles involved, Australian Pony Clubs meet up for inter-branch gymkhanas and competitions

possible there – ponies like the dark colt born on the hillside of the Awatere valley some sixteen years ago. For five years he ran wild, unapproachable and defying all efforts at capture. Then, glimpsed by a prospective buyer, he was at last run into a specially built stockyard, and tamed and trained after a battle of wits. Even now fences and five-foot-high yards will not hold that pony if he has the mind to jump out but Tosca, as he was called, became an award winner for the Marlborough Pony Club, competing often at championship level and never once eliminated.

In the early days when mounts were easier to come by, several members of the Kaikohe Riding Club, the forerunner of the Hawkes Bay Pony Club, bought ponies very cheaply. A quiet, all-purpose animal could be obtained from the local pound for a nominal sum, and at least one pony obtained from this humble source won prizes for jumping in many shows. Miss Prim, another of the same club's star performers, was originally caught on the gum hills by the Maoris.

At twenty-five years old Jimmy, the patriarchal pony member of the Hamilton Pony Club, has been ridden by four families of Pony Club children. He is still very much in demand and like Nancy, the chocolate-coloured little mare that takes pride of place in the

Pony Clubs teach young riders to rest their ponies between events

Rodney Pony Club, specializes in giving small children confidence.

Many Australian children, whether or not they are numbered among the 22,600 Pony Club members on the continent, do ride ponies although the family stock horse or ex-racer is often handed down to the youngsters as a matter of course. This an ex-British Pony Club member discovered to her embarrassment when she turned up at a rally to film part of a programme devoted entirely to ponies, and discovered the whole ride gallivanting gaily on enormous horses. Ponies are sometimes an advantage at a rally when, instruction finished with, the mounted games begin. A handy pony can really move fast during the quick changes of direction demanded in the popular pastime of barrel racing.

In such a vast land there is inevitably a need for different types of Pony Club branches, suited to the climate and conditions of their particular regions. Around Melbourne the turn-out is smart, the emphasis on eventing, jumping and dressage, and an overall high standard. The inter-branch championship, with forty or fifty teams competing has developed into a two-day affair since the Pony Club began in that area in 1948 – and there has been an incredible improvement in both riding and horse and pony management since those early days.

Australian Pony Club members receiving instruction on jumping

Gymkhana ponies, Pony Club or not, need to be nippy, obedient and of placid temperament

Up-country, the standards may be dissimilar to those of the more sophisticated clubs, but the fun is as good and the instruction sensibly geared to local needs. The saddle cloth may be the ubiquitous sack and the bridle may be held together with string but so long as the result is adequate, no member is made to feel his tack is inferior, and there is quick praise for a clean supple saddle, however old. One aim of the Club is to get the ponies into thick snaffle bits instead of the formerly popular pelhams. As in England there is a special Pony Club saddle, selling reasonably to members, but many children utilize a scaled-down stock saddle, and the sole aims are safety for the rider, and comfort for the pony.

Around many of the cities ponies are hired from riding schools, or kept in the same unaccommodating conditions as in New Zealand. The country ponies are all kept at grass, and hundreds of horses and ponies are grazed in small paddocks among the lovely riding country of the Dandenong Ranges around Melbourne – the relatively cold temperatures of winter and night-time defeated by the use of New Zealand rugs.

When the harsh heat of a Cyprus summer softens first to sunny autumn days, then to winter rains violent enough to turn parched fields to quagmires, an incongruous sound echoes at intervals through the orange groves. For twice a week from September until January, the cries of hounds and the notes of the huntsman's horn announce that the Dhekelia Draghounds are running a line over

Members of the West Norfolk branch of the Pony Club setting out for a ride

the rocky ground – maybe to follow a scent through the higher scrubland, to kill among the sand dunes on the western shore.

It takes a bold pony, locally bred, to keep up with hounds on a good scenting day, when the pace quickens over stones and boulders, and the jumping includes artificial fences as well as the native hazards of old slit trenches, unmarked wells, and the odd roll of overgrown barbed wire. The majority of the field, mostly British servicemen and their families, ride these local animals and this certainly applies to members of the four Pony Club branches, affiliated to the Akrotiri, Dhekelia, Episkopi and Famagusta Saddle Clubs.

Once they have passed their 'Grade C' test, Pony Club members hunt whenever feasible, as well as using the ponies – native cross-breds with a strong Arabian flavour – for every possible Pony Club activity. Few children possess their own, and the Saddle Club ponies present some difficulties, especially for novices. Many of them come from the Nicosia racecourse which normally ensures a 'puller', or from farms where they have been used for carting. Despite these slight snags, and a climate that sizzles in summer and that can be both wet and cold in winter, the Cyprus Pony Club continues to flourish. Most activities are crammed into the Easter holidays, gymkhanas enlivening the routine of working rallies, and the weeks are highlighted with treks up-country culminating in barbecues and beach parties which make enjoyable conclusions

The Taunton Vale Pony Club branch team circle the ring in triumph after their victory in the Prince Philip Cup

to any riding diversions.

Malta's sun-baked rocky surface does not sound like a horseman's paradise, but the Maltese are a nation of horselovers as well as being keen racegoers. There has been a branch of the Pony Club in Malta for about fourteen years, the enthusiasm of the members largely dependent on that of the various British Army officers who by custom act as District Commissioners. After an interim when the Club became almost non-existent, steady interest and progress has been building up since 1965. Now with seven instructional rides a week, there are classes catering for all standards from beginners to advanced. A popular summer school has now replaced the camp that used to be held in the grounds of the Governor's summer palace at Verdala. It begins at seven o'clock in the morning, the best time for riding in a hot climate, with four hours in the saddle followed by lectures, stable management, tack cleaning, and necessities such as clipping and bandaging. The week ends with an oral examination in the form of quiz competitions, riding tests, competitive games and a most welcome tea party by the swimming pool.

The Pony Club rides out at intervals throughout the year, but since the narrow roads carry much traffic and grass is unknown

Members of the British Pony Club acting as standard bearers to the following teams at the Royal International Horse Show

from May to October, these excursions are normally confined to the paths and tracks criss-crossing the Marsa – a large, flat and low-lying area encircled by the one-and-three-quarter-mile racetrack.

The Marsa is the hub of all riding and other sporting activities in Malta. In addition to bridle paths and several schooling manèges for the horsemen, there are tennis courts, sports pitches, a golf course, and the United Services' Sports Club swimming pool. The Polo Club – the oldest in Europe, having celebrated its centenary in 1968 – also operates on the Marsa.

Members of the Pony Club ride polo ponies belonging to the Combined Services Saddle Club. These are spirited creatures ranging in height from 13·2 to 15·3 hands, imported mostly from North Africa and possessing both Barb and Arabian blood. They combine the admirable qualities of fast galloping and turning like cats on the hard-baked ground when playing polo, with making excellent instructive material and behaving wonderfully well with children. Even the stallions have such good temperaments that some will go quietly on a leading-rein with a small beginner.

Every Pony Club has to adapt to local conditions and interest. In Jamaica the enthusiasm is not very great, but a camp 4,000 feet

A unique Pony Club in Germany, the members all aged between 8 and 12 and mounted on small ponies, give displays based on cavalry ceremonial

up in the Blue Mountains is something few members would care to miss. Especially when getting there entails riding a two hour trek up precipitous mountain tracks, where laughing children flock from huts to encourage the cavalcade, and where cooling streams plunge off the mountainside to the gullies far below.

When Mrs Bromley started a Pony Club branch in Asmara, Ethiopia, stable management was a problem just as it is in Denmark, but for a different reason. Not many Danish children attend boarding school and so most have much free time so that members of the relatively few Pony Clubs want to ride every week of the year. When they attend a rally they expect to actually ride, only a minority being willing to spend time on what seems to them to be rather remote theories on looking after ponies which do not belong to them. Activity, riding out and jumping are what they want.

The Ethiopian, Italian, American and British members of the Asmara Pony Club were lucky enough to have the use of an arena specially constructed in the palace grounds. However, with restrictions imposed by homework and a land where the sun always sets early, their time with the horses and ponies was limited. No ponies were privately owned but the Emperor, himself a fine

horseman, loaned three Lipizzaner mares which, with good
Arabian stallions from the Yemen, helped to make up numbers.
Owing to the difficult terrain, hard, stony and full of hazardous
cracks, the schooling and most of the riding was confined to the
palace arena. Here mounted games were always a popular diver-
sion, especially when the Imperial Army Band could be persuaded
to come and play for musical chairs on horseback. There were
occasional Sunday picnics when Pony Club members, divided into
two parties, borrowed horses from the Imperial police force for
the more experienced riders, to supplement the loaned royal horses
and miscellany of native ponies. They rode out into the country in
force, to be met by parents transporting the essential provender,
and returned replete and happy just before darkness, when the
fierce heat of the sun had cooled.

Many countries send some of their Pony Club members on
exchange visits, when they have the chance not only to see how
other people live, but also to test their riding ability under strange
conditions and with unknown types of horses and ponies. In 1969
fifteen-year-old Hilary Harman of the Isle of Man Pony Club, was
nominated for a visit to the Rand Hunt and Witkoppen branches
of the South African Pony Club. Riding each day from seven
o'clock in the morning, in sunshine so brilliant it tanned her black
boots brown, Hilary was schooled in jumping by the famous
Micky Lowe. She also had the luck to compete in the inter-
territorial Pony Club horse trials at Kyalami, against other teams
from Britain, Zambia, and Rhodesia, as well as the home trained
South African teams.

It was the first time she had competed in a horse trial and Hilary
was loaned a Welsh pony called Taffy. She was placed reserve
champion as an individual, completing a two-and-a-half-mile
cross-country course with twenty-four jumps including several
twelve-foot drops and a swim across a lake.

*Dutch Pony Club members demon-
strate the versatility and strength of
their Shetland ponies*

Several German Pony Club members visited England in 1968,
some to go into camp with the Wilton Pony Club, some with the
Bicester branch. When four British boys travelled to Germany on a
return visit, they were all mounted on magnificent large horses,
including the eleven- and twelve-year-olds who looked proud, if a
trifle over-horsed, on 16·2 hand animals. By way of contrast, the
three German children who had camped with the Bicester branch,
all did extremely well in the first German one-day Pony Club horse
trial, riding small New Forest ponies.

Altogether there are 806 branches of the Pony Club in countries
overseas, and a further 208 in the United Kingdom. Between them
they provide instruction, fun and healthy competition for around
75,000 boys and girls under the age of twenty-one. The entire
organization stemmed from a scheme of 'sub-branches' started by

A jumping lesson over natural obstacles in a Pony Club paddock

Chiddingfold Farmers Branch of the Pony Club learn how to tackle painted fences

the British Institute of the Horse in 1928, and a year later the Pony Club proper was born. By 1930 there were 700 members in Britain, and the Royal Calpe Hunt Pony Club in Gibraltar had the honour of inaugurating the first affiliated overseas branch.

Almost every Pony Club branch was closed down during the last war, making a break of six years. It says much for the enthusiasm of the committee, and of the needs of young and old alike to get out into the fresh air with horses and ponies again, that the Pony Club resurrected and grew to its present strength.

The backbone of the Pony Club is the working rally. This is where the ordinary members, up to seventeen years old, and associate members between seventeen and twenty-one, learn what the Pony Club originally set out to teach. They discover how to ride correctly, with safety for themselves and comfort for their ponies; how to look after a pony in sickness and in health; how to school and get a pony fit both for ordinary riding together and for competitions; what tack to use, how to ensure it fits the pony, and how to look after it.

Pony Club officials are there to offer sympathetic advice to inexperienced owners of difficult or unsuitable ponies and saddlery. Instruction at working rallies is tempered with the fun and relaxation of mounted games, where the emphasis, as in all Pony Club competitions, is on the team and not on the individual. The majority of British Pony Club members have their own ponies, but many hire from riding stables, and those that come on foot are equally welcome. Everybody, whether consciously or not, imbibes something of one Pony Club precept: 'To promote the highest ideals of sportsmanship . . . thereby cultivating strength of character and self-discipline.'

The Pony Club caters for practically all forms of riding, competitive or otherwise. Members are taught road sense, stressing both the care and courtesy necessary for riding in modern-day traffic. Most branches have an annual camp or week's school, and go on mounted expeditions. The majority of British branches bear the name of their local hunt and support it, and Pony Club members can take tests in hunting and country lore. Headquarters are shared with the parent body, the British Horse Society at the National Equestrian Centre in Warwickshire. Here the extensive library includes a list of moderately priced publications on most aspects of pony and horse management, and there is access to the British Horse Society's extensive film library.

The Club fully supports the Duke of Edinburgh's Award Scheme, and co-operates with organizations such as the Boy Scouts, Girl Guides, The Youth Hostels Association, the National Trust and National Parks Commission. Members are actively engaged in helping to preserve the horsemen's ancient rights of

A splendid pyramid formed by ponies and riders of a German branch of the Pony Club

way – those bridlepaths and pack trails that still criss-cross the British countryside. They are also taught to respect the farmers' and landowners' property and interests.

For those interested in polo, many Pony Club branches will provide an introduction to the basic principles of the game. For the proficient, there are annual polo tournaments for both seniors and juniors, in which interested branches may enter a team.

For those whose ambitions lie in show jumping, most branches organize their own gymkhana or show, in addition to the area show jumping competition – for which the first and second winning teams of each area compete in a championship, usually held at the British Jumping Centre at Hickstead.

Some people consider that the competitive side to the Pony Club in Great Britain has grown out of proportion to the original aims – which concerned the ordinary rider with the average pony. In a few branches this may be true, but the hope of getting into a team for a competition such as the inter-branch annual horse trials acts as a spur to young riders. Furthermore, the area trials and eventual championship undoubtedly provide a real test of all-round riding ability, allied to the correct and systematic training of the pony. Riding in a competition that includes three tests, dressage, cross-country and show jumping, fosters courage and determination – both in those aspiring to be chosen for a team, and in those who compete on the day.

With his Pony Club mounted games competition, Prince Philip has provided for the ordinary family pony ridden by children who do not necessarily aspire to the heights of horse trials or show jumping. The games are all team events, ingenious variations on basic gymkhana races. The branches compete in regional meetings and zone finals, the winning teams enjoying the excitement of the championship, held at the Horse of the Year Show in October. The ponies are seldom very high-class or valuable creatures, but to succeed they have to be well trained, obedient and nimble, and their riders active and enthusiastic horsemen. The championship is always a most thrilling and popular part of the Horse of the Year Show, and it is a pity that the occasional criticism of 'rough riding' is sometimes justified. A will to win is essential, and in the heat of the moment it is easy to forget principles of good riding, but yanking at a pony's mouth is ugly, unacceptable and if the pony and rider are properly trained, totally unnecessary.

The Pony Club has its detractors and inevitably there is room for improvement in some directions and within individual branches. But where else will one find a world-wide organization, run almost entirely on a voluntary basis, that caters admirably for the needs of 75,000 young riders and their horses and ponies, drawn from all walks of life?

Acknowledgements

Colour plates
Godfrey Argent: 74, 78 and back jacket, 79. Australian News and Information Service: 126. Barnabys Picture Library: 19. Camera Press: 50, 74 top, 93 top. Nicholas Meyjes: 115. Miles Brothers: 96 right. New Zealand National Publicity Studios: 51, 127. Okapia Frankfurt: 55. Photo Researcher: 23 bottom. Prado Museum: 75. Syndication International: 23. John Tarlton: 50. Nicholas Toyne 85, 92, 93 top, 96 left. Guy Withers: 114. Z.F.A.: front jacket, 18, 22, 54.

Black and white
Jack Adams: 99. Animal Photography: 30. Godfrey Argent: 31 top, 52, 65 top left, 70, 71, 72, 76, 77 bottom. Australian News and Information Service: 31, 91 right, 124, 128, 129, 130-131. Bavaria Verlag: 14, 139. Barnabys Picture Library: 62 top. Bundesministeriums fur Land und Forstwirtschaft, Vienna: 16. Camera Press: 12, 28. Judith Campbell: 33, 40, 46, 83, 90 top, 104, 111, 112, back jacket flap. Findlay Davidson: endpapers. Jerome Dessain: 87. Eastern Daily Press: 80. Exmoor Pony Society: front jacket flap. Fox Photos: 41. Barry Griffiths: 56-57. Illustrated London News: 42-43. Kentish Express: 82. Kent Photos: 100. Keystone: 69. Leslie Lane: 58 bottom, 106, 134, 135. J. H. M. Lindeman: 137 top, 137 bottom. Gretar Oddsson Ljosm: 10. Malta Govt. Tourist Board: 45. Les Mayall: 63 bottom. Miles Brothers: 13, 15 bottom, 20, 107. Mrs Jane J. Miller: frontispiece, 9, 17, 21, 25, 31 bottom, 86, 88-89, 90 bottom, 91 left. Mirror Features: 36 bottom. Monty: 108, 113, 116. New Zealand High Commission: 105, 118, 120, 123. Desmond O'Neill: 77. Nordisk Pressefoto: 62. Ontario Department Tourism and Information: 34. Tom Parker: 49, 26 bottom. Photonews: 63 top. Pictorial Press: 64-65. Pony and Lighthorse: 47, 58 top, 109, 119 left, 125, 132, 133 left, 133 right, 140 top. Popperfoto: 44. Radio Times Hulton Picture Library: 66. Tony Ray: 89 top right. Riding for the Disabled Association: 36. T. Ryder: 65 top right. John Staehr: 98 bottom. Straits Times: 122. Syndication International: 27, 38, 39, 97. John Tarlton: 13 right, 53. Thames Television: 48. Sally Ann Thompson: 29. The Times: 37 top. John Topham: 15 top. Nicholas Toyne: 87, 102, 103. United Press International: 119 right. Thomas Wilkie: half-title, 24, 26 top, 61, 94, 98 top, 101, 105, 110, 138 bottom.